Praise for **The Biology of Leadership**

"This just might be one of the best, most practical, needed leadership books ever written. It's chock-full of real-world insights that can help anyone be a better person and leader in any context, however challenging. I wish every leader I've ever worked with could have had this book available to them to move from theory to practice to mastery. Highly, enthusiastically recommended! A real treat and a joy to read."

TOM MORRIS, philosopher and bestselling author of over thirty pioneering books, including *Philosophy for Dummies*

"Carl Oxholm's approach to leadership development is practical, passionate, and insightful. If you want to effectively lead with authenticity and positivity, *The Biology of Leadership* provides all you need to succeed on your learning journey!"

JOHN BIANCHINI, global chairman and CEO of Hatch

"Masterfully simple yet highly inspired in its lessons, *The Biology of Leadership* is the playbook for how to better understand and care for yourself and your influence on others. It is a must-read for anyone looking to be a force for good."

MELAINA VINSKI, MSc, PhD, associate client partner, behavioral science and AI & analytics, at IBM

"*The Biology of Leadership* prepares us to embark on an extraordinary journey to explore the heart and soul of becoming an authentic, influential, and empowering leader. Carl Oxholm will guide you toward becoming the best version of yourself."

LAUREN JAWNO, director of coaching at Growth.com

"Carl Oxholm has outlined the key elements of leadership that leverage biological principles to bring out the best in yourself and others. These key values can create energy and an environment where all can give their courageous ideas and constructive insights."

JAMES BAIN, MD, MSc, FRCSC, professor of plastic surgery at McMaster University

"In a world where we must do more with less, juggle competing priorities, and thrive in a competitive environment that is ever-changing, Carl Oxholm shows us how we can take back control of our experience by arming us with strategies to intentionally lead with humanity."

LIZ BOUTHILLIER, SVP of sales at Franklin Templeton Investments

"*The Biology of Leadership* walks you through what you need to know to be a strong and responsible leader who drives profitability and contributes to meaningful organizations."

TATIJANA BUSIC, PhD, CPsych, clinical and organizational psychologist at Busic Psychology & Consulting

"*The Biology of Leadership* helped me to reflect on twenty-five-plus years of my (good and not-so-good) leadership practice and will be my guideline for many years to come, as a leader who thrives by serving with love, heart, and courage."

ROBERT HARDT, president and CEO of Plasma Water Solutions Inc.

"*The Biology of Leadership* is a remarkable book that's brimming with practical information. I'm now aware of how our collective biology impacts our thoughts, attitudes, interactions, work, and, most importantly for me, our creativity."

DAVE BEATTY, partner and creative producer at Secret Sauce Entertainment Inc.

"*The Biology of Leadership* is an extraordinary gift that encompasses not only what it means to be a present, compassionate, and aware leader who brings out the best in people and the organizations we serve, but also provides the keys to becoming the best version of ourselves."

AMINA DEIAB, CEO and founder of QED Inc.

"*The Biology of Leadership* has unpacked remarkable nuggets of wisdom that actually make it simpler to be, and to contribute, our best. It will guarantee our path to more effective leadership."

TAHIR AYUB, EVP and CFO at OpenRoad Auto Group

"Carl Oxholm provides us with an excellent reminder of how we can interact with everyone in our lives to help ourselves and the people around us achieve maximum potential."

JOHN JEFFERSON, SVP–controller at Carnival Cruise Line

"*The Biology of Leadership* is the real deal and a gift to the leader in all of us. It is an eye-opening and valuable reference, and an important reminder to pause and reflect on your own actions and their impact."

GAYLE HOEY, partner at PwC Canada

"Carl Oxholm has written a book that clarifies how leadership is truly a whole brain, whole heart, and whole body experience. By missing any of these elements, we run the risk of seriously shortchanging those who rely on us to lead."

ANDY MARTINIELLO, executive coach, leadership development facilitator, and board director

"Through captivating storytelling, Carl Oxholm creates magic as he delves into the science of human biology and applies it in a way that will leave you with the knowledge and confidence to traverse your own leadership journey to greater heights."

LI ZHANG, MBA, PMP, principal of corporate citizenship at CPA Canada

"For anyone struggling to achieve an outcome, become more effective, lead better—all while enjoying the ride more—this book will speak directly to your soul."

CHRIS WILLIAMS, senior strategy consultant and host of Badass Agile

"Carl Oxholm is challenging our basic beliefs of the importance of our emotions. We feel before we think—and this is the foundation of why we do what we do."

CARLOS DAVIDOVICH, MD, professor of neuromanagement at University of New York in Prague and author of *Five Brain Leadership*

"*The Biology of Leadership* captures Carl Oxholm's unique philosophy and approach to humanitarian leadership and living an authentic life. This is the type of positive, human-centric leadership that we are all craving."

SHELLEY M. WHITE, MA, CEO of Responsible Gambling Council

"*The Biology of Leadership* is a must-read for anyone looking to improve their leadership skills and become more effective."

KHALED SULTAN, senior portfolio manager at CIBC

"Carl Oxholm demonstrates his human approach to leadership by emphasizing the whole person and what they experience, so a leader can appreciate the importance of these concepts and be truly present for those they lead. Finally, a leadership book that I couldn't put down!"

GINO SCAPILLATI, vice chair of strategy and innovation at Bennett Jones

Embrace Your Human Nature and Become a Better Leader

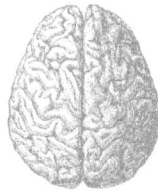

THE BIOLOGY OF LEADERSHIP

CARL OXHOLM

Foreword by **MICHAEL BUNGAY STANIER**

Cataloguing in publication information is available from Library and Archives Canada.
ISBN 978-1-77458-355-5 (paperback)
ISBN 978-1-77458-356-2 (ebook)

Page Two
pagetwo.com

Edited by Scott Steedman
Copyedited by Kendra Ward
Cover and interior design by Jennifer Lum
Interior illustrations by Fiona Lee

virtuecompass.com

To Julie Oxholm—your light guides my every step,
fills me with hope, and inspires me to always give my best.
This book is a celebration of the love, wisdom, and
support that you, Scott, and Haley give me every day.
From my heart and mind to yours—thank you!

Contents

Foreword
Out of Your Mind

F OR THE longest time, I assumed my body was just a convenient container to carry around my brain.

I'm definitely one of those more cerebral types. I love wrestling with ideas, and I've made a good life by teaching and translating them for people. I love strategizing and thinking about the future (too often at the expense of being present in the present). In short, I spend a lot of time in my head. If you hold a leadership role in an organization, perhaps you do too.

Some years ago, I heard an insight that tilted slightly the axis of my world: "The body leads the brain." Huh. So, it's more than just a brain transportation device? Apparently so. Here's how it works. If you want to be confident, shifting your body into a confident stance primes your brain to understand that you're feeling confident right now. If you want to be curious, know how to set your body up in "curious pose," and your brain will follow suit. If you want to be present, know what it takes to regulate your breathing and set your posture in "present mode," and your brain will get the hint.

Here's one way that's changed things for me. I've now got two small desks in my office. One I sit at to be efficient:

answer emails, take calls, do the managerial role that's required of me. The other I sit at to be in maker mode: writing books, designing programs, writing introductions to books written by friends I admire, and so on. One desk sets my body up to think one way. The other desk sets my body up to think another.

Carl, whom I've known for over twenty years, has taught me an expanded iteration of the "body leads the brain" insight. The body leads the room. Which means the body, your body, your biology, leads the organization.

Culture and Strategy

As a leader, you know well the eternal dance between culture and strategy. Even though, contrary to popular belief, Peter Drucker never actually said "culture eats strategy for breakfast," we all understand that there's no point in having a business plan without the right people executing it, in the right way.

Your organization's culture includes things outside your direct influence, such as the org chart, the values, the color the walls are painted, how hybrid working works, and how meetings get run. It also includes your actions (and inaction) as a leader. You can't simply think or act your way into great leadership. It starts with how you are as a leader, the "being."

Taking a Stand

Carl and I met when he was a lead partner at one of the world's largest professional services firms. My company Box of Crayons had been hired to help shift their coaching culture.

Carl was asked to lead the project because he was . . . a little different. Sure, he had the chops to be a great tax guy and lead complicated accounting projects. That's not what made him different. He stood out because he focused on how to bring out the best in the people around him: his team, his clients, his peers, and his colleagues. He's always been relentless about building his own capacity as a leader, both through his own learning and through the way he's role modeled and taught others the wisdom you're about to read in his book.

Finally—and this is what I most admire—he's been unflinching about holding the line and taking a stand for this work. When people didn't understand, he persisted. When people got angry, he remained unruffled. When people finally saw the light, he generously said "sure thing" rather than "I told you so."

If you're looking to take a stand in how you show up as a leader, and if you're looking to take a stand on what modern leadership needs to be in our organizations today, read on. I'm confident *The Biology of Leadership* will be the book for you.

Michael Bungay Stanier
bestselling author of The Coaching Habit *and recipient of the 2023 Thinkers50 Coaching and Mentoring Award*

Introduction

ARLY ON in my leadership coaching journey, I was asked to propose a coaching development program to a client's board of directors. As they neared the end of two full days of meetings, I was the last speaker, slotted in at 4:30 p.m. on a Friday. I was wondering what their energy level would be like. The night before, my wife asked me if I was nervous.

"Excited," I replied, and then I admitted that I did feel the weight of my team's hopes that an effective presentation could bring us more meaningful work. I added that I could see one of two possibilities: Either the board would be welcoming, appreciative, encouraging, mindful, and focused on the opportunity of the program, or they would not. If the former, the conversation would have its best chance to flow creatively and naturally; if the latter, perhaps I could use their reluctance as evidence to convince them that they could use our help. I'm not sure I fully believed the latter possibility, but it did help me sleep well that night.

When I arrived the next afternoon and observed my upcoming audience, I could see they were all much older and more experienced than I was; this was a very experienced group of leaders. No welcome, no warmth, no apparent appreciation. Having arrived during the final break of their day, I was simply told to connect my computer and get ready to present.

By now, most of us have likely heard about the need for psychological safety if we are to access the best of our intellect, but this board obviously had not received that memo yet. Moreover, when they reconvened, the CEO started by saying, "Carl, we're tired and ready to go home, so why don't you scrap the slides and just cut to the chase?"

Experience has taught me that nothing succeeds like a challenge. I was anxious, but the challenge was not what concerned me. I sensed that their exhaustion and apparent frustration with one another might erode their willingness to consider the program I was there to discuss. In that moment, I was afraid that the hopes and great intentions of my team would be dismissed before we even started.

We can all relate to being emotionally hijacked—let's call it "incapacitated" for now—and this was one of those moments for me. The good news was that, even back then, some of the research I'll discuss in this book was available to me, precisely when I needed it most. I knew what was happening to my mind and body, so I paused, took several conscious breaths, and asked some logistical questions to buy myself a little bit of time. As my brain came back online, the question that I needed to advance our discussion hit me just in time. "So," I asked, "how do any of you know when you're doing great work?"

One of the fifteen senior board members spoke first. "Carl," he said, "are you about to tell us we need to be positively reinforcing one another? Because if that's the case, I'll save you some time. You see, at a certain level of leadership, you no longer need any of that."

I smiled and said, "Actually, I was just wondering how any of you know when you're doing great work."

The CEO spoke up: "If we're being honest with one another, then no news is good news. At our level of leadership, the problems all bubble up to the top. So, if we're not hearing anything, or we're not hearing much, then we know we must be doing great work."

I asked the rest of the room what they thought, and one by one they all fell in line.

Still breathing deeply and consciously, I asked another question that popped into my head. "Thank you for everyone's input. So, if no news is good news, then when do you typically communicate with one another?"

Another member chimed in, "Only when there's bad news."

"Congratulations," I said. "There's your culture. Intentional or not."

One of them immediately (and audibly) smacked their forehead and said, "Wow, I just realized something. Since we teach and train our staff to find exceptions, that's how we also lead our people—by exception. They only tend to hear from us when there's a problem."

"Sounds exhausting and not much fun," I said, smiling again. "When you look at the mission, vision, and values of your organization, do you think that this approach will most effectively get you to where you want to go, and in a way that attracts, engages, and motivates your people?"

This question was met with a long and heavy silence. Finally, one of the board members asked me what I thought. I opened my computer and pulled up a slide that detailed their mission, vision, and values. I reminded them of the highlights and then asked the same question again. The room broke out in laughter.

"Laughter can often be telling," I said once it subsided. "Would someone like to interpret it?"

Another member said, "There's no chance we can argue that our current habits will most effectively close the gap between where we are and where we say we want to be, so let's not even suggest it."

We were hired.

Hone Leadership Skills with Practice

Leadership is a skill (some might even say a lifestyle), not merely a decree bestowed from on high. Despite the board members' remarkable experience in formal roles, their lack of self-awareness and social awareness was notable—and not all that uncommon. Luckily, their humility saved the day. They used our exchange and the months that followed as an opportunity to turn their individual and organizational lenses inward, learning to walk their talk more consciously and to reinforce the behavior that aligned with who they wanted to become.

Despite their seniority, these board members had not been aware of their opportunity—even responsibility—to create an environment conducive to guests offering them their best. And until we broke down some of the barriers between us with honest questions and a desire to listen to one another, we risked only hearing from one or two board members and losing the value that was eventually shared from multiple diverse perspectives.

This brief story asks us to face any number of questions. Such as:

- How important is it to set the right tone for creativity to thrive?

- How confident are you that you are not contributing to someone else's incapacitation?

- Do you consciously practice encouragement, to increase the odds of everyone gaining access to their best?

- Did you know that seniority can sway the room and snowball conclusions, cultivating a yes-person culture?

- Do you ever consider how your self-expression affects others?

The list goes on.

So many similar meetings conclude without everyone experiencing the best of one another and benefiting from what each person has to offer. We can do better, and we need to do better, if we are to tap into the remarkable potential that exists in every voice.

That meeting highlighted a dual passion of mine: to better understand how to self-regulate my emotions, in order to give myself and others the best chance possible to offer our best; and to experiment with optimizing the quality of the energy in any given room, so that everyone present wants to share their best. Years later, this same passion gave rise to my pursuit of a professional coaching certification and ultimately served as the foundation of the services provided by the company I started, Virtue Compass, Inc. The need for this assistance will long outlive me—but in the meantime,

We feel
before we think.

I will be honored to support all who share this passion for creating more meaningful (and pleasant) experiences with one another.

Hence, the essence of this book: the art (and science) of mindfully affecting the quality of the experiences we cocreate with one another.

Which leads to a finer point. What actions, demonstrated with consistency, will maximize higher-quality, more positive impact? There are experiential clues and scientific insights everywhere. That's what I want to share with you now.

Why the "Biology" of Leadership?

How can we optimize the positive influence we have on others? If, as research shows, the quality of our relationships is the number one determinant of our holistic health and well-being, then this question is an important one for leaders. And if we layer on the finding that how we influence others starts with how effectively we influence ourselves, then the path to healthy growth, progress, and success—for ourselves and for all within our sphere—becomes clearer.

Perhaps our habits are not what they could be, the results we're influencing in others not optimal, our quality of performance inconsistent—this would not be unique to anyone. So what can we do about it? In *The Biology of Leadership*, I distill what I've learned over my many years of leadership experience and share some insights that I hope can be useful. The stories are mine; the science is everyone's; and the lessons learned are yours, should you choose to experiment accordingly.

Understanding the biology of leadership is empowering because it promotes a new level of self-awareness and positions you to successfully self-regulate, manage, and lead yourself. Psychology, sociology, and philosophy are fantastic too, of course. But I like to start with biology because it's something we all share. It's fundamental to who we are, and it applies equally to all of us. Several times in this book I will say, "We feel before we think." On my leadership journey, realizing this was my first big "aha" moment, one that shaped my practice. In the corporate world that I've been playing in for more than thirty years, this lesson was profound—especially since most companies behave as though feelings are "things" best left at home.

Unregulated emotions force us into a reactive survival mode, even when this is not our desired state. The fight-or-flight (and freeze or faint) reaction has its time and place, but we want to keep it under control when we're not facing an existential threat. Our physiology does not know the difference between an actual threat and a perceived one. So, if we're not self-aware, we risk shutting down our best available capabilities at the very moment we need them most.

Looking back on that board meeting, it's clear to me that if my incapacitation had lasted, if my frozen state had precluded me from being engaged and accessing the essence of what our team wanted to offer, none of what followed would have happened—which would have been unfortunate given the success our program went on to bring to the organization.

Then came the realization that the scientific communities and the faith-based communities, who don't always see eye-to-eye, seem to agree on one core notion: Everything is energy. As I explored this concept, three key questions arose:

* What is the quality of your energy?
* What is the focus of your energy?
* And what is the expression of your energy?

These concepts will be explored in great detail in this book. As I played with these questions more and more, the science and the experiential insight revealed some wonderfully effective practices.

I discovered another insight too: Life rewards action. Many of us tend to believe our way into action, but we can also *act our way into believing.* Olympic athletes know this well, but for many in the corporate world, the practice of it often proves elusive.

Although I appreciate that the science will continue to grow, be clarified, course-correct, and so on, one starting point will remain constant: learning to be more consciously a student of our own experience. Every one of us is an original, a one of a kind, never to be again. My hope is that you see yourself in some of the stories or scientific insights in the pages ahead, and experiment with the choices you feel and think will best serve you and those in your care.

This book will help you understand how our biology guides us to our best, binds us with one another in our common humanity, and equips us to ensure our practices align with our conscious, best versions of ourselves (and not the unconscious, suboptimally programmed alternative).

Whether expressing the human side of being or the being side of our humanity, we need more honest, transparent discussions about the things that get in our way, and their opposites: the conscious actions that enhance our experiences and that encourage others to come to know their best.

Because of my experience in numerous leadership roles within the corporate community, I've been told that this book must be for that exclusive audience of current and future leaders. Perhaps, but my family has also assured me that these insights, tactics, and techniques have helped them and their friends too. So, I write this for anyone who needs a friendly reminder that you matter, that you truly are a biological wonder, a one-of-a-kind expression of life itself; if we don't get to experience who you truly are, everyone loses.

Would you say that you work to live or live to work? How about a different alternative: live to live? As an integral part of life, work is about facing challenge, learning, deepening understanding, being heard, being seen, being valued, being appreciated—having fun—and, of course, feeling that you're contributing value in service of something bigger than yourself.

So, live into the answers (as my mother would say) and see how, as a student of your own experience, you are in the best position to know what choices will make the greatest positive impact for yourself and others. Doing this habitually will allow all of us to benefit, more often than not. Evolving is not about perfection; it is about progress—in a direction that feels right, that you enjoy, and that you explore with others who appreciate you, celebrate you, and want to cocreate for the benefit of all involved. I hope you enjoy it!

PART I

BIOLOGY SUGGESTS THAT HOW YOU FEEL MATTERS

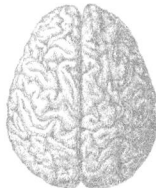

1

Biology and Leadership

ISA, A senior VP at a large multinational company, hired me to give a keynote speech on the importance of leadership and emotional intelligence in the workplace. The next day, she called me back, apologizing profusely. Yes, I'd already been hired, but could I come in tomorrow for a second interview? Her boss was now insisting that *he* be the person to decide who to hire.

"Sure," I said. Appreciating how awkward this was for Lisa, I added that I would be happy to meet again and told her to not give it a second thought.

The next day I arrived about ten minutes early. Lisa was there to greet me and we had a lovely conversation as we waited. Her boss, Henry, finally arrived, fifteen minutes late. He was clearly flustered. "Why are we here again... and I'm sorry, you are?" he asked.

Lisa looked as though she wanted to crawl under the table. Clearly embarrassed by Henry's behavior, she shifted from relaxed and engaged to anxious and uneasy.

I smiled and introduced myself, while thanking them both again for the opportunity to have this conversation. About twenty minutes into our discussion of my keynote, Henry suggested that he understood what Lisa and I had agreed to but wanted to be convinced more pragmatically. "Make this real for me or it's not happening," he said.

"Sure," I replied. "I have a question for you." As Henry leaned forward, I asked, "How conscious were you of the energy you brought into this room when you sat down in front of me, your guest, and Lisa, your highly valued colleague?"

He looked at me and said, "Come again?"

I repeated the question.

"Well, if I'm being honest..." He paused.

"Please," I said.

"I was not conscious of my energy at all. Not really."

I thanked him for his honesty and then asked, "With that in mind, how conscious are you now of the effect your energy is having on me, your guest, and Lisa, your highly valued colleague?"

Shifting in his seat a bit, he replied, "Not very." He then looked at me and said, "Have I adversely affected you because of how I entered the room?"

"Me, no." I chuckled. "But that's because I'm used to this."

Henry then turned to Lisa and asked her the same question. She froze for a moment and then quietly replied that she was OK—except her face had turned several shades of bright red, and her eyes, open to their widest, looked at us with trepidation. I gently brought Henry's attention back to me by suggesting that if they hired me, he'd never have to ask that question again.

I had just one more question for Henry. "If the person you report to was 100 percent conscious of the energy they brought to every interaction they had with you, would you consider that a good thing, a bad thing, or would you be indifferent?"

He laughed, looked at Lisa and then back to me, and said, "You don't know who I report to?"

"I don't."

"Well, I report to the chairman of the board... and frankly, if that were the case, it would be a dream."

"And there you have it," I replied. "For you, it would be a dream for your leader to show up conscious of the energy they bring to each interaction, and yet, by your own admission, you haven't made the same conscious choice to do that for those who report to you."

He paused for a moment and then reached out his hand to shake mine. "You're hired. On one condition. Please assure me that you'll speak with my executive team like this. We're not accustomed to these types of conversations."

Before he excused himself, Henry asked me one more thing. "Carl, if I pause before entering my next meeting, reflect on the quality of my energy, and attempt to be more conscious of its influence, are you telling me that alone will have an impact?"

My response: "Yes, although there's no need to take my word for it. Being a student of your own experience, run the experiment and observe what happens."

"I will," he said with a grin.

Henry called me at the end of that same day. He had run the experiment and was pleasantly surprised that such a seemingly small practice could yield such meaningful results.

But to go back to our meeting, before he left, Henry apologized to me and to Lisa for how he had entered the room and for not being more conscious and respectful. Lisa later said of this acknowledgment, "Wow. Simply, wow!"

HENRY'S INITIAL behavior is all too common—and I imagine that most of us can recognize and empathize with Lisa's discomfort.

Think of your own work life. Have you ever felt highly distressed when your boss walked into a meeting? (If your answer is yes, in other words, if your boss is your focus of concern or worry when they enter the room, then they are no leader. They are simply someone in a formal position of authority who does not understand or appreciate the inspirational opportunity afforded their privileged role. Translation: They're bad for business.)

Have you watched your colleagues give up their unique points of view and acquiesce to the authority in the room?

Have you seen the dynamic shift away from present-moment awareness and high-quality energy to muted voices and conformist attitudes?

Why is it that so many leaders incapacitate the very people they need to perform at their best, precisely when they need them most?

Everywhere I travel, I meet wonderful people, and most understand the need to be heard, valued, appreciated, and cared about. And yet, so often, I notice how their courage and integrity can be compromised when they work in teams. Time and time again I see how important leadership is to the energy in the room—both in how we conduct ourselves and, in turn, in how we influence others. Ultimately, if we do not walk our talk, others won't believe us; as we'll see, this will start a domino effect involving attitudes, emotional states, actions, and results.

Think about it this way. Rather than focusing their energy on the issue at hand, people are focusing on the mood and presence of their leader, and whether they seem approving

The leader in you will outperform earlier versions of yourself to the extent that you better understand how your biology affects your ability to offer your best.

or not. This dynamic is costly to the business and to the collective pursuit of its stated mission.

Our business community has long held that rational thought should dictate everything we say and do. This makes sense, but only as long as we can access the best of our intellect, consistently. And since, biologically speaking, we feel before we think, we can only be guided by steady, rational thought if we are aware of our emotions and can manage them accordingly.

An abundance of new research is shedding light on the way our brains work in relation to performance and behavior. In this book, I draw on some of these key insights from neuroscience, and years of leadership experience, to help us better understand why we do what we do. I focus on the relevance of biology to business, so that leaders become more intelligent about their emotions, optimize their influence, and more consistently play to the win-win. The leader in you will outperform earlier versions of yourself to the extent that you better understand how your biology affects your ability to offer your best. That's the promise of this book.

My work with Lisa and Henry started with the keynote and progressed to workshops that helped the executive team ask ongoing questions, report back on what was working, share key learnings, and consistently focus on what they wanted instead of complaining about what they didn't. They established routines to start meetings more effectively (for example, always beginning with the organizational mission statement to provide context for decisions), agreed on the attitudes expected during these meetings (for example, prioritizing top challenges and achievements rather than framing for problems and threats), and developed a way to close that ensured everyone's voice was heard and respected.

After discussing many of the concepts outlined in this book, the executives better understood how they were getting in their own way and adversely affecting others on the team. They practiced being more intentional about their attention and learned to shift from *talking* about their values to consciously *modeling* them. Perfectly? Of course not. But more optimally today than yesterday. Our work together helped the executive team focus on improving their interactions with others—and on measuring the improvements.

The team learned to assess how intentional they were with each interaction—consciously practicing key values or rubbing their decisions up against the company's mission to check for alignment, and even its vision to check on direction. Like most companies, theirs had two key areas for development: culture work (affecting behavioral norms) and strategy work (making sure they were moving in the same direction, with a clear understanding of why). Both were necessary.

All this work created a positive, meaningfully sustained shift in behavior that was exhilarating for everyone on Henry and Lisa's team. It was a tremendous success for the organization, not just in the moment but as an extension of how they designed their strategies and developed their leadership program. And the cascading effect was profound. I received ongoing feedback, and they all said, "Wow, that was really different. It was necessary, and in the long term, brand-defining." Perhaps this positive impact is not surprising. After all, the etymology of the word "identity" is "consistency of beingness"—so when behavior becomes more consciously and consistently aligned with stated values, the positive impact on the brand follows.

In the process, I learned that Lisa is an incredible executive. Her energy and her enthusiasm are literally contagious—

as long as she allows them to radiate, authentically. This can be true for all of us. Highly infectious, yes, which leads us to another question: Are you mindful of how you infect others? With possibility or with fear? Until it was pointed out to him, Henry was not aware of his impact. He's a good person who had worked with Lisa for years. He had just never recognized the connection between who she could be and who she showed up as every day: the person she became in his presence.

Henry needed help recognizing that disconnect so he could overcome it. The wonderful part is that he was open-minded enough to explore what he couldn't see and cared enough to do something about that. It's never too late to start. Or, said another way, "It's always day one."

Setting the Stage

Biology: The word "biology" is derived from the Greek words *bios*, meaning life, and *logos*, meaning study. It is the science of life and living organisms. For our purposes, it encompasses the physiology, behavior, and other qualities of a particular organism: you.

Leadership: According to *Forbes*, leadership is a process of social influence that optimizes and maximizes the efforts of others toward the achievement of a goal. To which I would add that if you want to positively influence another and optimize/maximize effort, then leadership must start within. In other words, how effectively you influence and lead *yourself* will determine how effectively you influence and lead *others*.

This book explores how our biology affects our ability to lead ourselves and those in our care. With this understanding, we increase our individual and collective effectiveness and actualize untapped potential so that all team members, including ourselves, can perform at their best. I've often heard it said that "team" is an acronym: Together, everyone achieves more. This can certainly be true when we better understand our biology and choose to consciously practice optimizing the quality, focus, and expression of our energy (much more on this in coming chapters). Synergy is real—we can cocreate a whole that is greater than the sum of its parts. But one plus one can also equal minus three if we're not conscious of the impact we're having on one another. Ever been in the presence of someone who has the habit of creating a toxic multiplier effect? Unfortunately, I'm guessing that for many of us, the answer is yes.

We feel before we think. As I alluded to earlier, exploring and understanding this scientific insight changed everything for me. I spent almost thirty years with one of the largest professional services firms in the world, spanning many roles while taking on local, national, and global leadership responsibilities. I've been led by many, I've been asked to lead many, and I have always been fascinated with how to be at my best while helping others do the same.

Science and experience continue to teach me that only once we become more aware of how our emotions impact our performance can we access the best of our intellect. As more research becomes available, I am reminded of how our biology informs our ability to progress. And I am convinced that more leaders, particularly in business, would benefit from a cogent summary of key scientific insights into how we influence ourselves and those we have the privilege to lead.

That's why I wrote *The Biology of Leadership.* Too many business leaders blithely ignore their impact. Too many dysfunctional habits have created the foundation of a culture that does not serve its citizens as well as it could. The number of times I have heard "leaders" say that business is business and personal is personal, and never the twain shall meet, is mind-numbing. A whole person (and thereby a whole leader) inhabits every waking moment, so let's not pretend (or pressure) otherwise. Too much potential untapped and too many moments of discontent—we're better than that. This book is about how to bridge this disconnect.

To add emphasis: Why the reference to biology? I like the way Yuval Noah Harari puts it in *Sapiens*: "Biology sets the basic parameters for the behavior and capacities of *Homo sapiens*. The whole of history takes place within the bounds of this biological arena." If we are to become more effective leaders, we need to understand how our biology informs our capacity to access our best.

2

Inside the Biology
of Leadership

ECENT RESEARCH in neuroscience has helped us understand our biology more effectively, but I've found that there are still few sources that parse the learning so that we can make constructive use of it in business and beyond. So, let's explore the biology of leadership together.

With Lisa and Henry from the previous chapter in mind, let's better understand what was playing out, biologically speaking, during our meeting together. This involves taking a closer look at how our biology impacts our capacity to think. This can be a game- and life-changer.

Here is a scenario. Our ancient ancestor, let's call him Gary, was on the hunt when suddenly life happened—in the form of a saber-toothed tiger that, out of nowhere, pounced. Without thinking, Gary instantly fled, because his life depended on it. Still to this day, when we encounter a physical threat, like Gary did, our body instinctively kicks us into survival mode (which under the right circumstances, like Gary's, is a good thing).

What happens? Well, when the physical threat manifests, cortisol (our body's primary stress hormone) floods the thinking part of our brain and sends adrenaline and blood to the big muscles in our body. You may be familiar with the terminology that typically attaches to this occurrence: Our biology has just prepared us to either fight or flee, to survive. Interestingly, when we become active, the cortisol dissipates, which eventually allows us to think clearly again.

So, why explain this now? Because not everyone knows that our bodies react the very same way to a *perceived* threat as they do to a *real* threat. The instant we perceive a threat in our midst, our thinking center is literally incapacitated. That email in bold or all caps or limited grammar that you just received, that voice message in a tone you felt was threatening, or any number of scenarios and countless more could trigger you. Even those of us who know about the fight-or-flight reaction don't always appreciate that we've just been triggered toward incapacitation. Either way, becoming more aware of this reaction can be helpful.

Furthermore, did you know that two additional *f*'s accompany the possibility of fight or flight? We may also freeze or, in more extreme situations, faint. Imagine you're in a not entirely welcoming boardroom, in the middle of an important presentation to a prospective client, and they ask you an unexpected question that could threaten the success of the deal—you get triggered. Access to your greatest ideas slips away as your prefrontal cortex is suddenly flooded and incapacitated.

I don't recommend that, in that moment, you reach across the table and fight the person who asked the question; nor do I recommend that you abandon your laptop and run out of the room (something tells me that may undermine their

INSIDE THE BIOLOGY OF LEADERSHIP **29**

confidence and trust in you). But your body still needs to cope with what's happening, and the cortisol isn't stopping. This is when you'll likely freeze (or, in extreme cases, faint).

Any lawyers reading this may be familiar with legitimate defenses such as temporary insanity or crimes of passion. We can be so incapacitated that we're not even held legally responsible for our actions. Recall that when Henry entered the room the way he did, and then questioned Lisa and me the way he did, Lisa was emotionally hijacked. I could see it in her stunned expression, red cheeks, and agitated posture—she was in no position to access the best of her intellect in that moment (explaining her one-word answers when questioned).

Also worth noting: The written word carries with it a multiplier effect when it comes to emotional incapacitation. Why? Because absent the physical cues and tone of voice we get with speech, everything is left to our own imagination. As I heard Deepak Chopra once suggest, our imagination can only serve one of two purposes: It feeds our creativity, or it feeds our anxiety. The good news is, as the preferred option the next time we feel anxious, we can pause, recall the flip side of the coin, and get creative.

A Word about Fawning

As a brief aside, although I've focused my discussion on fight, flight, freeze, and faint, be aware that another trauma response, fawning, is also an automatic reaction for those who needed (and developed) it for their survival.

Fawning was recently identified by psychotherapist Pete Walker. It occurs when people try to please others at the expense of their own needs, rather than confronting (fight), running away from (flight), or blocking out (freeze) a threat. Fawning is often associated with PTSD or complex trauma that occurs during childhood. As Gregory Jantz explains, complex trauma is "typically perpetrated by someone who was supposed to care for you (like a parent or a caregiver). When a child is abused repeatedly by a caregiver, they may develop attachment problems later on in life. They can also learn to go into the fawn response, since children aren't able to fight or flee in their daily lives."

Fawning behaviors may include someone apologizing for things they didn't do or holding back their opinions to not upset others. In the workplace, you may see it in someone who appeases a boss to try to avoid upsetting them.

When *another* becomes more important than oneself, any number of unfavorable habits can result. Understanding this can be the first step toward healing, self-compassion, and attuning to values and boundaries. Not to mention promoting an awareness of being more selective about the company we keep.

THE LIMBIC SYSTEM AND PREFRONTAL CORTEX

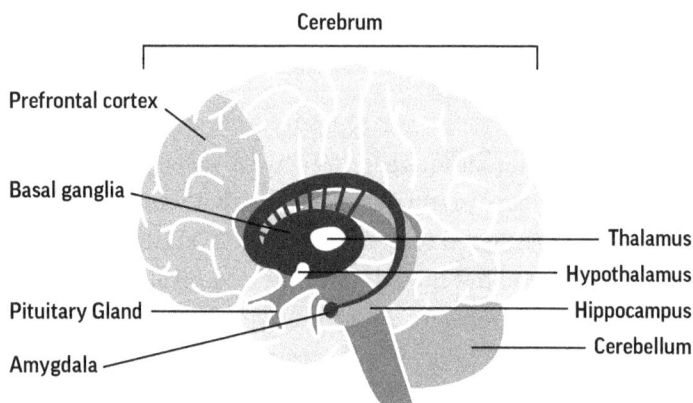

Cerebrum

Prefrontal cortex

Basal ganglia

Pituitary Gland

Amygdala

Thalamus

Hypothalamus

Hippocampus

Cerebellum

Emotional and Thinking Centers in the Brain

So, what's the picture of the brain on page 30 all about? Again, keeping it very high level, let me just say that the complex section that sits atop our spinal cord is our limbic area, a set of structures in the brain, which houses our emotional center. As we take in the world through our five senses, the signals we receive travel through the limbic area en route to our prefrontal cortex (our thinking center). Hence that axiom you now know, we feel before we think. And emotion arises as our feelings arise. In other words, feeling a particular way is an internal state that we may express externally via our emotions.

Put another way, our current emotional state has a direct causal relationship with our capacity to think. Perceived threats that trigger survival instincts render us incapacitated and less capable of accessing the best that our analytical brain has to offer.

Think about that. Any outside influence that we feel *has the potential* to be a threat may decrease our thinking capability.

This matters why? Well, we all want to think and perform well—and this simply isn't possible when our emotions get the better of us. Consider the businesses that rely on their people being at their best (only all of them), providing the best solutions for their customers, creating the best experiences, and demonstrating the highest-quality service. All of which will be compromised if those people can't access their insights, training, and experience.

WHEN I was with my previous professional services firm, we did some work with a retired four-star general in the United States military. I asked him, "General, what's your favorite go-to when it comes to developing others?"

We're designed to operate at peak levels of thinking proficiency by seeing the world through a compassionate lens.

He said, "Carl, that's easy. When under duress, we default to our level of training."

Equipped with this insight, I've since asked many a leader, "If you take a company that espouses its values, which are intended to represent the behavioral expectations of its brand, but its people never consciously practice modeling their values, then when under duress, what is their likely default action, individually or collectively?"

After some consideration, they often share a similar reply: "Well, I guess it's just whatever they know and/or feel in the moment."

Unless you practice otherwise, when the pressure is on, your default is going to be whatever your thoughts are in the moment (as an extension of your emotional state). In other words, if you're a hothead, you're going to get hotter.

The bridge from theory to mastery is practice. Do you practice choosing words and actions that align with one or several of the values you (and/or your organization) espouse? Only those of us who consciously practice this can rely on a default position that represents the best of our values in action. And a company can only be values driven if its people consciously practice living its values—particularly when times are toughest. The leader in you, of course, will always start with yourself. This is one way to ensure you author the best of who you can be—and do so by design, not by chance.

When I ask executives if they agree with the four-star general's observation, they all nod yes. So, I ask them, "Knowing this, how trained are you in living your values, behaviorally speaking?"

This is important because countless formally appointed leaders among us have no idea about the biology of their own leadership. If, at the eleventh hour, things are at their most challenging and the pressure is on, that's precisely when our leaders need to be *at their best* to ensure that we remain *at our best*. And yet we know many leaders who "turn the screws" and "crank up the heat" when the pressure is on.

To them, I say this: If your teams perceive these actions as threatening, then you've just succeeded in incapacitating the very assets that you are responsible for leading, and at the very moment when their best is needed most. This doesn't sound like strong leadership to me.

Leaders with these unconscious tendencies are leaders in title only. The best leadership requires an ability to create resonant relationships that strengthen one's influence in a constructive, supportive, effective way. Absent a level of self-awareness that allows you to self-manage (and lead) accordingly, your influence will be hit-and-miss. So too the consistency of your results.

Let Love Rule

Our survival instinct is terrific and serves us well when *true* survival is at stake. This instinct has evolved over thousands of years, so once triggered, there's no getting around it. But we can influence how *often* it's triggered. I've learned that context shapes our perspective, which in turn shapes our perception (and therefore our reality). Since our perspective (the lens through which we see the world) influences our perception, let's focus there.

We all *choose* our perspectives. So, tell me, what do you think happens when we see the world through what I'll call a loving lens? Or if "love" is too soft a word for you, how about the compassionate, mindful, hopeful, optimistic, constructive, or supportive side of the spectrum? When you view the world through this perspective, what do you think happens to the emotional center in your brain? The answer is that it works in harmony with your thinking center. This points to the fact that we're biologically hardwired to be loving creatures. That's not a Hallmark card. It's true: We're designed to operate at peak levels of thinking proficiency by seeing the world through a compassionate lens.

Some of you may have heard that we have three brains and that we optimize our holistic health and well-being if we start with the "heart brain" (more on this in chapter 4). Without even having the benefit of more detail yet, you might understand how this could establish the foundation for your "head brain" to perform at optimal levels, thus allowing your creative expression to thrive. The leader in you knows this.

So, if a loving lens is on one side of the perspective spectrum, what do you think resides on the other side of the spectrum? If you guessed fear, you guessed right. Fear may also be experienced as resentment, bitterness, jealousy, envy, hypercompetitiveness, and so on. Unfortunately, this is the predominant paradigm for many. So, if your tendency is to see the world through a lens of fear, what then is the relationship between your emotional and thinking centers? Fear constantly triggers the amygdala (the integrative center in your brain responsible for emotions, emotional behavior, and motivation), activating an emotional hijack and shutting down the thinking center (by flooding it with cortisol). Why? Because, as you now know, your body thinks it needs to prepare for fighting or fleeing (or freezing or fainting).

What I love about this discussion is how it brings everything together. The heart brain is the best place to start, and it helps you access the best of your thinking capacity. I also find it fun to talk about because in business we rarely hear about the importance of being more intentional about our attention. If your personal (and corporate) values do not align with some aspect of the loving side of the spectrum, then be aware that your lens may not serve you (and those around you) at optimal levels of performance and productivity. The fear-based side of the spectrum breeds a scarcity mindset that is bound to be triggered frequently, thus leaving you compromised.

3

The Emotional Hijack

TYPICALLY AT this point in any group workshop or keynote I lead, I like to pause and recap what we've learned so far. But rather than doing it myself, I prefer to randomly select someone to do it for me.

Imagine this. We're in a conference center and you and I are just two of the one thousand people in the room. I've been facilitating a conversation that covers a great deal of what I have shared with you so far in this book. I then say, "I'm sorry I haven't had the opportunity to meet all of you in person yet." As I'm saying this, I'm walking around the room and between the tables, holding a microphone and looking everyone in the eye.

I go on, "This is a fun part of the conversation where I get to prove the current slide—'Each and Every One of Us Is Brilliant and Unique'—to everyone here in attendance. You may think it's just a nice slide with a friendly comment, but it speaks the truth. If only we would all believe this, then we likely wouldn't need to dig into the details of what we've been covering. Why? Because we would find it perfectly logical to simply contribute the best of ourselves in each moment for the benefit of others and ourselves.

"Nonetheless, here's my ask. When I pick one of you, please share the top three points that you have found most informative so far. But I also want you to add a fourth point, your own pearl of wisdom that helps you when times are most challenging. Here's what I can promise you: Every time I've done this, the pearl is incredible. So, thank you in advance for agreeing to share your genius. Now, let me pick someone to stand and share their thoughts with the room. Oh, and just think, we're so fortunate that the cameras recording this event will capture your every word."

I continue to walk around the room—and believe me, this is the only time during the day when I lose the eye contact with literally everyone. I then reach out... This is where I want you to imagine that I have just selected you. So, tell me, how do you feel standing in front of a thousand people, microphone in hand, with the cameras rolling?

If you're like everyone I've ever done this with, you've just uttered an audible "ugh," followed by laughter and an expression that reads, "*Nooooooo*, please not me." But relax. I immediately let you off the hook by saying, "It's OK. I've changed my mind. Rather than what I had originally asked, I have one simple question instead. How's your pulse rate right about now?"

Laughter ensues and invariably the person shares that their pulse is racing, plus they're feeling flushed, warm. Some encounter shallow breathing. The list goes on. I'll often ask how many people in the room were happy or relieved that I did not pick them. Again, more laughter as everyone raises a hand. That's when I say, "So, what just happened?" Thanks to our previous discussion, they all know the answer—the emotional hijack just occurred.

The SOS Technique

As much as you may want to contribute from the best of your experience, to the extent that you've been hijacked, you can't. Your wonderful knowledge and intellect remains, of course. The trouble is, you can't access it. Emotion takes hold, and you're prone to react instead of reflectively respond. Life happens, and then you have a brief moment (or two) to choose how to respond. The greater your self-awareness, the greater your opportunity to produce a high-quality response. Between an external stimulus and your response is a moment in time, and the quality of your choices within that moment will determine the quality of your leadership. When you have limited to no reflective thought between stimulus and response, you are likely to react out of pure emotion. You are apt to do and/or say things that you later find yourself apologizing for.

How can you perform well if you're struggling to think clearly? Hijacks are getting in the way of high performance.

Have you ever heard of the ninety-ten principle? I first heard famed author Stephen Covey speak of this (and the related research). It goes like this: 10 percent of life experience stems from the fact that "life happens"; the other 90 percent stems from how you react (or preferably respond) to the 10 percent. This is why being aware of your triggers is so important. If you can witness what's happening physiologically, you can become empowered to do something constructive about it.

Imagine you are operating at a high level of self-awareness and recognize that one of your triggers is being pulled. Then what? Let me share what some of the athletes I once worked with shared. It's called the SOS technique:

Stop

Oxygenate

Seek information

So why stop first? Because, being aware of your body's own distress signal, you know that your capacity to think clearly has been compromised. So, you stop. You do not say or do anything when triggered but rather respect that others could benefit from your best.

Then oxygenate: Breathe. Why? Proper in-and-out, through-the-nose breathing can activate the parasympathetic nervous system (PNS), which helps you remain calm. As Sanjay Gupta shares, "One of the reasons that deep breathing is so effective is that it triggers a parasympathetic nerve response, as opposed to a sympathetic nerve response, the latter of which is sensitive to stress and anxiety. When you perceive stress, the sympathetic nervous system springs into action, resulting in surges of the stress hormones cortisol and adrenaline. The parasympathetic nervous system instead can trigger a relaxation response, and deep breathing is one of the quickest means of getting there. In a deeply relaxed state, your heartbeat calms down, breathing slows, and blood pressure lowers."

That's why Navy SEALs are trained to make conscious breathing their number one go-to when facing a threat. Oxygen helps the body reduce the cortisol that is flooding your prefrontal cortex. We're hearing more and more about the importance of taking deep breaths and now we know why. This takes practice, but eventually you can learn to observe your emotions and consciously breathe as a matter of course.

Then seek information. In other words, ask questions. Why? First, because the questions buy time (while you continue to breathe deeply). You are preparing your brain to be able to access the best of its storehouse of information. Second, asking questions allows you to clarify. Recall that context shapes perspective, and more information can help you reframe more accurately. Perhaps you were making assumptions (and those very assumptions were the main reason for your hijack). Questions (and curiosity) serve as an antidote to arrogance and also help ensure that, before you seek to be understood, you are first clearly understanding the other person. There's no greater gift than to ask someone else their thoughts. So, start giving.

Try practicing the SOS technique the next time you are in a stressful situation. Knowing your emotional triggers can also be helpful. We have four primary emotions: glad, sad, mad, and scared. As a student of your own experience, you can learn to recognize when your buttons are being pushed (you're being triggered) and become mindful of any corresponding impact on your emotional state. Your specific awareness will help you determine when to use the SOS strategy.

And very importantly, know this: Only you can activate your buttons. When my kids were younger, I often would joke with them and suggest they save their energy because I disconnected my buttons a long time ago. It's akin to understanding that while I know I can't control everything that happens in my life, I am 100 percent in control of my response.

So, you may be wondering if we do not activate the SOS technique when we are triggered, how long before the cortisol will dissipate on its own? Apparently, it's approximately fifteen to eighteen minutes. An eternity in business. We often don't have that much time when critical decisions are required.

But if you can be fully present, you can de-emphasize the story and allow the experience to unfold in real time, avoiding a hijack. That's why practicing being mindful can be a game-changer.

An easy tip for how to practice this is to focus your mind's attention on following your body. In other words, wherever you are physically, practice being there mentally. Do you think you're good at this? Most of us are terrible at it. We're almost never where we are. We're ruminating about moments gone by or anxious about the ones still to come.

Interestingly enough, memories are just current thoughts about the past; and thoughts about the future, likewise, can only happen in this present moment. In the present moment, we are free of past and future thoughts if we train ourselves to stay focused on the *now*. I've heard it said that a wealth of information leads to a poverty of attention. Mindfulness allows us to train and condition our brain to stay here, now, in this moment (or, at the very least, more often). Upset about something? Notice that, unless it's a physical threat, your thoughts about the matter may have the greatest consequence. Is it possible for you (the leader in you, perhaps) to look at the situation through a different lens and come to a more constructive conclusion? The moment "is as it is," but your feelings and thoughts about it can shape your experience accordingly. As can your perspective. How would the leader in you think about the issue? And how would the leader in you respond? What are you telling yourself about this moment?

Did you know that we're all fortune tellers of sorts? Show me who you are now, in this moment, and depending upon what you model, I can basically tell you what your life will be like in the future. Simply put, the quality of my current moment is always the next best determinant of my future self. Again, this is not about ignoring dire threats. Of course, we need compassion to address hardships that are literally about

Each and every
one of us is brilliant
and unique.

first securing our survival. Beyond those life-threatening moments—and hopefully most of us will experience very few of these—it may be helpful to befriend *this* moment. It's the only one we will ever have.

YOU REALLY are brilliant and unique—simply because you are. If you understand this, then your behavior will align with a harmonious state (except when your instinct needs to step in to save you from an actual, not just a perceived, threat). But a perceived threat can impact you just as significantly, especially if in the midst of it, you remain unaware of being emotionally hijacked.

Have I ever conducted the experiment of singling out an audience member and observed someone who isn't hijacked? Not exactly. Whenever I have performed this with people in the same room as me, 100 percent of the time they acknowledge the fear and a similar end result. On one occasion, I was in front of a live audience and a large audience over video call and dial-in. I decided to choose one person in the room along with one from the list of call-in attendees. When I asked the individual on the phone how it felt to be selected, their response was "I'm just fine, thanks." And although the shake in their voice betrayed their words, they suggested an interesting result—when not visible to others, many feign calm in the face of panic.

There are two ways to avoid the hijack: (1) be open, curious, hopeful, compassionate, positive, and optimistic; and (2) have a significant ego and don't care about what others think. Why? Because the hijack results from a perceived threat. So, the first strategy allows us to remain centered and reflectively responsive such that what we have to share may be helpful (knowing that it comes from our authentic, original self). The second strategy holds the opinions of others as less important, so the threat is insignificant.

Also note that someone with less experience is more likely to be hijacked. This is most often explained by their having limited life experience to draw upon (less context), and so less ability to reframe and maintain a constructive perspective. Perhaps now you can see why a breadth of experience is so valuable to the ongoing success of any team or organization.

Jim's Request

This last point reminds me of a story involving Jim, a relatively new member of a client's team. The CEO, Jasmine, asked if I could make time for a coffee with her and Jim. On the day in question, Jasmine mentioned what a wonderful addition to the team Jim was. We were meeting because Jim had posed a question to Jasmine that they both wanted my thoughts on. Jasmine turned our discussion over to Jim and asked him to explain his point of view and his resulting request.

Jim thanked Jasmine and me, and then shared how thrilled he was to be a part of this amazing company, which he hoped to be a long-standing member of well into its future. I sensed a "but" coming, and sure enough, Jim said, "But I'm not sure that will be possible if we don't align around my value." I asked him to please elaborate and he said, "I've had a great deal of success helping the team reprogram for outdated code, and I think that, as a result, I should be paid comparable to my current boss. After all, he does similar work but makes more money than I do."

I shared that his thought process was not that uncommon and that, with his permission, I'd like to offer some thoughts on the matter. He sat up and listened attentively. I started by asking him, "Have you ever thought about how life is expressed as a series of patterns?" He said he had not, and so I explained. "I like to think of life's patterns as belonging to one of three distinct buckets. Bucket one is all about pattern recognition. As life starts out, we're faced with new patterns all the time, but with practice and experience these patterns become more familiar, thus allowing us to address them more efficiently."

I checked in to ensure this resonated and when Jim confirmed, I continued. "Once we become more familiar with certain patterns, we find it fun to focus our energy on pattern optimization. That's bucket two. It's one thing to recognize what's happening, and it's another to want to improve accordingly, for the benefit of all concerned." Jim nodded and I could see that he was still with me. "And then, having a solid handle on recognition and optimization, we arrive at the third bucket: pattern creation. That's where we take our wisdom and affect new patterns that serve a need. So, why do I say all of this? Because, you're describing being highly proficient at elements of bucket one with some contribution to bucket two and maybe even a little of bucket three. But if I understand correctly, you're saying that this may be true with respect to your current level of focus and responsibility. Is that a fair assessment?"

He nodded and said yes.

I shared, "So, if I pick a completely different type of challenge, one that you personally have never seen before—so no pattern recognition to speak of—but your current boss, Simon, has been there and done that many times before, how do you think you'll handle that challenge relative to him?"

Jim paused and then acknowledged that he would need to consult and likely research before knowing what the best course of action could be. In other words, he would need more time before acting.

I thanked him for his honesty and said, "There you have it. You see, experience—and pattern recognition, optimization, and creation—matters and brings tremendous efficiency and effectiveness to a business. So it's true, you may be on par with respect to your current singular area of focus, but Simon's incremental pay is for being battle-tested, so to speak. That extra time that you would need is time we could invest otherwise if our leader already knew what to do. Simon's broader-based wisdom is perpetually available for the benefit of the team, in the event that any number of previous challenges repeat themselves."

Jim had never looked at it that way before and said that he understood the value that Simon's broader experience brought to the table.

Because within this company I had already conducted workshops that explained some of the baseline tenets of emotional intelligence, Jim also recognized how that broader acumen would make Simon less likely to experience a hijack because, as I shared above, his experience would afford him a different context and, therefore, a greater ability to reframe for calm, thoughtful action. I concluded by asking Jim to guess about Jasmine's expanse of pattern recognition, optimization, and creation. His humility shone through as he celebrated her inspiring history and concluded with "Point very clearly taken and understood."

We often judge ourselves harshly and become defensive, thus triggering a survival instinct, resulting in self-preservation (a me-centric paradigm), good for true survival but less productive for everyday collaboration. Effective leaders establish a safe environment to voice opinions as their number one priority. Now we know why.

4

The Three Brains

WHEN I first heard about the findings that suggested we have three brains (that we know of), I was fascinated. As Grant Soosalu and Marvin Oka describe in their comprehensive research:

Starting with his pioneering research on neuro-cardiology, Dr. J. Andrew Armour introduced the concept of a functional brain in the heart. His work revealed that the heart has a complex intrinsic neural network sufficiently sophisticated to qualify as a "brain" in its own right. The heart's neural network meets all the criteria specified for a brain including several types of neurons, motor neurons, sensory neurons, interneurons, neurotransmitters, proteins and support cells. Its complex and elaborate neural circuitry allows the heart brain to function independently of the head brain and it can learn, remember, feel and sense.

Following on, neurobiologist and MD Dr. Michael Gershon published his pivotal book, *The Second Brain*, in which he described the culmination of over a decade of research and discovery that the gut also contains a complex and fully functional neural network or "brain." The gut brain, also known as the enteric brain, contains over 500 million neurons and sends and receives nerve signals throughout the chest and torso and innervates organs as diverse as the pancreas, lungs, diaphragm and liver. The gut brain is a vast chemical and neuro-hormonal warehouse and utilizes every class of neurotransmitter found in the head brain. Research has shown that it can learn, store memories and perform complex independent processing.

When I oversee workshops and present keynotes I tend to reference the conversation in this space as "bonus material," because new insights are emerging continuously. For now, at least, that we have three brains is not common knowledge. I've stood in front of thousands of people and asked, "Who here has heard that we have three brains?" and maybe 5 percent have raised their hands. And when I expand the question to add, "For those who just raised your hand, was it metaphorical in context—for example, the proverbial head, heart, and gut instinct—or do you mean physiological?" The response is consistent: 95 percent of the 5 percent say "metaphorical." Three brains . . . Really?

The science suggests that each of our three brains serves a specific intellect: In very simple terms, the head brain is responsible for our creativity; the heart brain, compassion; and the gut brain, courage. Do you think we access these brains in a sequence—first, second, and then third—every time? Or do you think our circumstances dictate when we access our creativity, compassion, or courage? Most people guess that the order is variable and circumstantial—but the science suggests otherwise. There appears to be an optimal sequence as it relates to our ability to perform at our best.

Soosalu and Oka's research suggests that we would be wise to practice always starting with our heart (compassion). Maybe not that surprising when we remember that we feel before we think. Why else might we start with compassion? In my experience, we would do this because resonance resides in the heart. In the business context we might refer to this as "rapport." It's all about connection, having each other's back, being on the same wavelength (we can even measure this now). One definition of leadership suggests it's about our ability to create a resonant relationship with another. As Richard Boyatzis put it in a Case Western University course I attended in 2013, "The best leaders build or rebuild resonant relationships. These are relationships in which the leader is in tune with or in sync with the people around him or her."

A compassionate lens bodes well for our ability to remain calm under pressure. This is relevant, especially since it can be said that our body is eavesdropping on our thoughts. When you think about it, our internal organs and cells don't have any direct access to the outside world—that's why the quality of "culture" they live in is so important. Our thoughts affect our blood's culture and its biochemistry. If you practice a lot of frustrating, angry, fear-oriented thoughts, then naturally you're going to produce quite a toxic soup. If instead you say to yourself, "I can figure this out. Practice empathy and approach yourself and others with compassion," you produce a healthier biochemical culture for your cells to thrive in. This is why thoughtfully considering your self-talk, along with your external expression, is so important. I recall one communication expert commenting that approximately 90 percent of our conversations are with ourselves—so we would do well to be more mindful of our word selection, internal tone, body language, and how all three can benefit from practicing a compassionate perspective.

ONCE WE have this meaningful connection, where to next? Well, when you're with someone you have this kind of relationship with, are you primed for open, free, and creative dialogue? Yes—or certainly more so than you would be if you were in a room with people you did not know or trust. It follows logically that you go to the head brain next. It's time to get creative. When you have a meaningful, high-quality relationship and a sense of rapport with your team member, you can tap into the best of your creativity in service of whatever is important now. This sequence positions you to optimize your imagination.

But we all know many people who have fantastic, high-quality relationships, terrific ideas, and yet nothing happens. So, we can't forget about our third brain—the one that helps us act, with courage. Life rewards action, so it's time to experiment. The word "courage" itself derives from "heart in action."

But let's not overthink this. Just use your sense of when to move from one brain to the next, and experiment with what is most effective for you and those you serve. No need to blindly believe. With your next interaction, respond compassionately first. Then, once you sense a mutual understanding, get creative and trade ideas, after which close with a discussion and choose to pursue an option. Practicing this sequence will allow you to see for yourself whether you'd like to continue starting with your heart brain.

A brief example. Following a workshop I gave with an executive team, the CEO called and mentioned that his recollection of our three brains conversation forever changed his relationship with his seventeen-year-old son. When I asked if he would please elaborate, he said:

> My son came home from school two days ago and was clearly distraught, on the verge of tears. I was working from home that afternoon, and when he realized I was in our home office, he came to see me. "Dad, I need to tell you about how terrible my day was and then I want you to tell me what to do." He told me about what had happened.
>
> I paused for a few seconds and remembered my three brains—and specifically your challenge to experiment. So, I started with my best version of compassion.
>
> "Son, I heard what you said and can only imagine how challenging that must have been."
>
> At this point he just stared at me and said, "Dad, just tell me what to do."
>
> I was not overjoyed in that moment because it became clear to me that I must have previously always told my son what to do instead of really listening and supporting him to help himself. I didn't waver though, and did not feel as though I should move on from my heart brain. I put my arm around my son and said, "I hear you, and I will share some thoughts. I just wanted you to first know that I can see why this must be hard."
>
> His response, while subtle, was wonderful. He leaned into me and said nothing. I'm not thrilled to say that, in that moment, I could not recall the last time I had shown that level of empathy and compassion. After a few seconds with my arm around him, I thought to myself, This feels like the right time to get creative, and so I took one of your other suggestions and said, "Let's come up with some creative options. You go first."

To perform at your best, you would be wise to practice always starting with your heart.

After trading a few ideas, something magical happened. All of the pain that was with him only minutes earlier had now given way to the process of finding a possible solution together. I could see him starting to enjoy the creative process of trading ideas with his dad. Then I knew it was time to lean on my third brain and I said, "So, with all of these options now available, let's talk about action." Life rewards action, I remembered. "Which option are you going to act on tomorrow?" After he responded, I noticed something else that was fantastic. He turned to me and, with a smile on his face, said, "Thanks, Dad. I feel better and I'm actually looking forward to doing what we discussed. And if it doesn't work, we can regroup tomorrow and discuss which of the other options might."

This CEO's last few comments to me were "Thinking about my three brains and putting them to good use—by being more self-aware, giving my own interpretation, and ensuring that I didn't stop until consulting each one—made all the difference."

This is a nice representation of how important it is to put what we learn into practice, not overthinking but rather trusting our intuition. Here's a fun way of thinking about it: Our instinct helps us survive, but our intuition helps us thrive. Intuition—our inner teacher—has a voice. Have you listened to it lately?

This also reminds me of the concept of the win-win situation: in other words, ensuring that our choices benefit both parties involved. If something is going to work well for you but someone else has to pay the price for your benefit, then there is a better option. Experience has taught me that you don't want to sacrifice yourself either. Nobody who truly cares about you wants you to do that. So, the lose-win isn't healthy or optimal. Let's instead practice staying creative and constructive as we cocreate options that work well for all involved.

Creating a Culture of Safety

In *Your Body Is Your Brain*, Amanda Blake discusses how the human brain has evolved over millennia. Its development started with safety: The reptilian part of our brain was all about the need to survive. Then, over time, we developed the limbic area, critical to our ability to form meaningful connections with others. And finally came the cortical brain, which gave us the opportunity to evidence respect. All of this development was critical for tribes to form and to elevate humans to the top of the food chain. Safety, connection, and respect.

When I first heard Blake speak about this from a neuroscientific perspective, I couldn't help but also think of it as a blueprint for effective leadership in business. Imagine asking, "Leader X, how do you create and evidence a safe environment for your people? One where they can thrive in physical, emotional, and psychological safety? How do you do that, consciously?"

The second component part is connection. "How do you evidence connection? How do you let someone know that you support them, believe in them, champion them, celebrate them, know them, appreciate them? Care that they're on your team?" All the things that really create the ties that bind.

And lastly, respect. History demonstrates that respect is necessary for a tribe to find harmony and coherence and, therefore, high performance. "So, how do you evidence respect?" If a leader condescends, bullies, or is unreasonable and unsupportive, then the person on the receiving end will clearly not feel respected.

How fun, I thought—here's this terrific neuroscientist talking about human evolution and perhaps not even realizing that she has just provided a terrific insight for effective leadership. Any leader who ponders and experiments with intentionally creating a safe environment, where connection is prioritized and respect is a must, will be well on their way to forming relationships that can be trusted, in a space where performance can flourish. This becomes obvious when we consider all that we've covered so far. Fewer hijacks, fewer unwanted surprises, greater collaboration, more fun, stronger bonds that last, and trusting relationships that underpin the promise of unselfish teamwork in service of something that matters.

Author Daniel Pink talks about another triad. He says motivation is the sum total of purpose, autonomy, and mastery. What fascinates me most is how these qualities interconnect. Interconnectivity makes these concepts stickier for executives. If you know your why—your purpose, organizationally— and you have command of your subject matter or area of expertise, well then, of course, I can allow you to have autonomy. If we're aligned on the why and you've got mad skills in a certain area, I can give you all the autonomy you want. There's this perfect, symbiotic, synergistic relationship between purpose, autonomy, and mastery.

I'll often ask CEOs, "Does anyone else know why you do what you do?"

"No doubt we could do a better job of that" is the usual response.

"And your people? Do they feel capable, competent, supported? Are they getting ongoing, effective coaching? What's their learning and development like, to attain mastery?"

And by the way, mastery isn't just subject matter expertise—it's behavioral. The neurons that fire together wire together. The more you practice something, the more myelin sheath forms. This is an insulating layer that encases nerves cells, allowing electrical impulses to travel faster and more efficiently. The more you practice, the more you create these sheaths, which can rapidly speed up your ability to do the skill that relies on that interconnectivity. You can multiply it to three thousand times the speed.

And remember mastery is also about what you practice. Are you practicing misery, or are you practicing possibility? Many people do not realize how often they focus on what they *don't* want, as opposed to what they *do* want. The more you practice focusing on what you want and align your wants with what your organization needs (its mission), the greater the autonomy that can be offered.

We saw that during the pandemic. There was tremendous push and pull around telling people what to do and how to do it. This kind of tension is not necessary if you've got deep, meaningful relationships. Once you establish a certain level of resonance and rapport, people don't want to let each other down.

5

What Has Experience Already Taught You?

Y OU HAVE LIKELY heard the phrase "soft skills." You've also likely been told that these are nice-to-have as opposed to must-have skills. But if I substitute the word "leadership" for "soft," all of a sudden, these skills come at a premium. So, let's explore what experience has taught us about the importance of emotional intelligence (EI)—that is, understanding how our emotions affect us and those in our care, the foundation of the so-called soft skills.

You're already well versed in EI and aware of its importance... Perhaps you just haven't realized this yet?

In his terrific *Harvard Business Review* article "What Makes a Leader?" Daniel Goleman suggests that leadership is composed of three domains of competence: IQ (intellectual capacity); technical skills (task-related skills, knowledge, and experience); and EI (managing emotions and building quality relationships). Many years ago, I decided to run an experiment similar to one performed by Goleman. First, I accepted his suggestion about the importance of IQ, technical skills, and EI. I followed that by posing a question to colleagues: "Think of the most inspiring and effective leader you have ever seen or known (real or fictional). What were their top ten attributes, the ones that made them so inspiring and effective?

THREE DOMAINS OF LEADERSHIP COMPETENCE

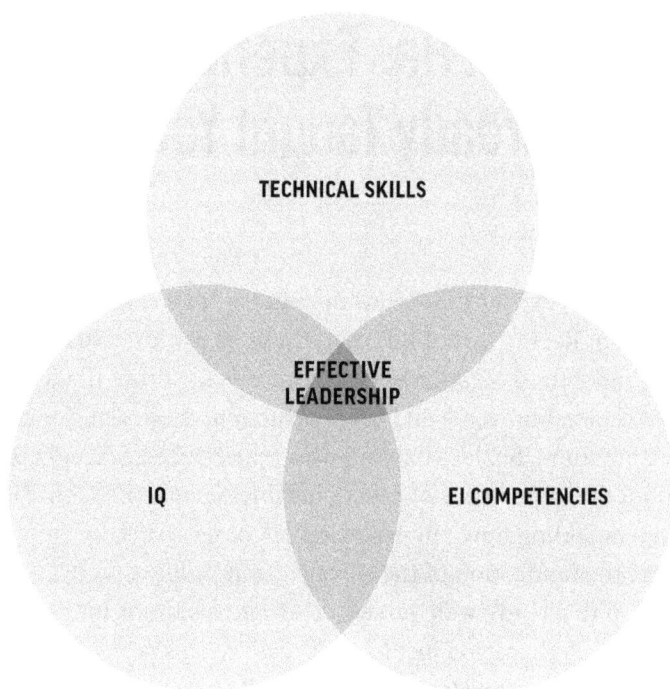

"Got it? Terrific. Now, write them down before we move on. OK, now let's vary the task. Think about the most toxic leader imaginable (real or fictional) and conduct the same exercise— what top ten attributes were responsible for their high level of ineffectiveness? While you might come up with some attributes that simply mirror the opposite of your first list, you may have additional insights too. Please write them down.

"So now you have two lists. One that describes the attributes of the most effective and inspiring leader and one that describes the most toxic. Next, look back at your lists and answer the question: Among these three domains of competence—IQ, technical skill, or EI—where do most of the attributes that you captured on your two lists reside?"

Try this experiment yourself. If you're like the thousands of people I've conducted it with, you will place the majority of the attributes—greater than 90 percent, with characteristics such as integrity, empathy, positivity, and adaptability—in the EI category. This result was consistent with Goleman's research. Why?

Firstly, if you have ever thought that EI doesn't matter or (like many senior executive leaders I've worked with) have muttered, "I don't get this EI stuff," you might find these results illuminating. I love asking people to be students of their own experience, because it's tough to lie to yourself. Even without any reference to neuroscience, our experience confirms that EI *does* matter. People around the world have agreed that they would prefer to work with (and for) leaders exhibiting attributes such as integrity, empathy, positivity, and so on.

From a self-awareness standpoint, do you see yourself in the first list? Do you practice being the source of what you seek, modeling the attributes that you would like to experience in others? Many have found it helpful to hold on to these lists and check in with themselves throughout the day to see if their actions align with the attributes they have chosen intentionally (while staying away from the attributes on the second list). This level of mindfulness and intention can transform your current reality and positively influence those around you.

Secondly, let me elaborate on the takeaway. I'm not suggesting for a second that IQ and technical skills are unimportant—they are important, critically so. But we all *know* that. If you take a room full of well-qualified executives, or team members of any kind, those who lead with higher levels of EI will create a distinctively beneficial experience. I remember being told that current science suggests our IQ is fully formed by the age of sixteen. If that's true, it means that no matter where you find yourself in life as an adult, the level of IQ necessary to perform in your current role is one that you *already have*. You are enough (so stop being so hard on yourself). Whether you demonstrated your IQ with your formal education, your interview skills, your work performance, et cetera, you must already have it, or you would not have made it this far. Why is this fact potentially profound? Because it supports that everyone on your team is capable, cognitively speaking—they just might not be competent yet.

Absent the requisite level of EI, thriving will prove more difficult. Knowing this changes the focus of leadership. How? Well, if I am leading a team and some members seem to be struggling, I know that their lack of comprehension is likely not a question of IQ, but perhaps has more to do with how I'm training, coaching, and approaching their needs.

What I love about this perspective is that it places the onus on the leader. I have often seen "leaders" who notice someone on their team struggling and get frustrated and suggest that the person must sort it out. With this new understanding, however, leaders might choose to adapt their teaching or communication styles to cater to team members more effectively.

Imagine developing teams whose members think that they're not good enough or smart enough. How many leaders who take responsibility for the effectiveness of their communication have you experienced? With this insight, that can change. You can assure your teams that they are capable and together learn to communicate in a tailored way that makes all the difference for everyone involved.

Many a CEO has shared with me that this insight made a meaningful difference. As one put it, "When a member of my team looked confused after I had shared a strategic imperative, I would feel frustrated inside and blame them for their lack of intellect or capability." She would vent to HR about their hiring policies and go on about "where have all the smart people gone" and "this isn't rocket science, what's wrong with these people" and "at this stage in your career I can't believe you don't seem able to grasp this..." And the list goes on. After reflecting on the interplay between IQ, technical skills, and EI, and accepting that each respective team member must already have the requisite IQ, the CEO now takes responsibility to bring everyone along. She's less inclined toward frustration and instead sees others' confusion as an opportunity to improve her own leadership acumen, close any gaps, and inspire team members to ask questions openly. This, in turn, has produced stronger teams because the quality of problem-solving is elevated. Team members are no longer afraid to voice their confusion. Indeed, it's where much of their innovation now comes from.

What kind of leader are you? How do you know?

Emotional Intelligence Differentiates

I was speaking to the leadership team at a boutique consulting firm the other day, and one of the team members happened to mention that their technical brilliance was their claim to fame. I asked, "Are you the only experts in your field who can solve the given problem being tabled?" They answered no. So, we discussed that, although they have the technical proficiency to solve problems, if the client did not enjoy the experience, how likely were they to come back? We agreed that the market will continue to explore until it finds those who can provide technical know-how and a pleasant experience.

The neuroscience shows that the degree of pleasantness of an interaction directly influences the emotion that it provokes, and that, in turn, affects our ability to think. When we empathize with others, they may give us access to some of the things that otherwise could have been cordoned off.

You think empathy is a soft skill? Expert negotiators insist it's a fundamental leadership skill. They call it "tactical empathy." Empathy is about understanding, and understanding targets our ability to serve and to puzzle-solve while negotiating effectively. In business, empathy is often the skill that separates you from the competition. Another firm may have bench strength that's just as deep as yours, but the team who really cares has an advantage.

I used to help some of my colleagues with audit proposals, listening to them prepare oral arguments. I would say to them, "You're hoping to win the opportunity to be the auditor of this company. So far, I've heard everything I need to know about why your audit opinion is of high quality and why it can be trusted. So, just so I'm clear, is that why we should hire you—because of the high quality and technically proficient opinion?"

Common reply: "Well, yes."

"OK, so when the other firms come in, are you suggesting that they're not technically competent? Would hiring them render exposure to a substandard opinion of the financial statements? Is that what we're implying with our approach?"

And of course, people would pause (usually while looking a little flushed) and answer, "Oh, no. No, we're not saying that at all."

"Then I still don't understand why I should select you."

My point was that the technical skills could be considered table stakes. The client already knew we could give a technically sound, high-quality audit opinion—otherwise, we would never have been invited to the table in the first place. During the proposal process, the prospective client wanted to experience what it was like to be around us. And if that positive experience could be replicated, on purpose, by design, with other people on the team, they would want more of that. That's why people will hire you.

"So to be clear," I would ask, "how much are you focusing not just on *what* you say but *why* you say it and *how* you're saying it? I want the why and the how to be as important as the what. Most around that table know about the what of your services. So, while it's important to mention, you'll rarely convince someone to hire you because of the uniqueness of your what. I want to know why you're doing what you do, and how you approach servicing the identified needs. And I want to experience what it feels like to team with you, how you work with people, observing whether your behavior aligns with your values. In terms of making my final decision, those are the differentiators."

Emotional intelligence is responsible for the strength of our underlying relationships—hence its importance when leading others and inspiring collaboration.

WE ALSO see the importance of EI when interviewing people for a position. Most companies still interview for technical acumen. Very few are adept at bringing the behavioral side of the equation out. People become enamored with grade point averages or the way someone looks and completely lose sight of how it is to be around that person, particularly when times are challenging.

And yet that's everything. You need to get past the script, because what you really want from an interview is to find out what it's like to be in a person's presence, especially when times are toughest. Because if they can meet that test, then, quite frankly, you can probably teach them anything. But do you want to be around them again? Getting past the stock stuff will take any number of queries.

Master negotiators are comfortable with silence, because they'll let you talk yourself right into a hole. Can a person dig themselves out? Sincerely and authentically? That's what matters. For most graduates today, the opportunities they are going to serve fifteen years from now don't exist yet. Technical acumen can matter, but it's also the easiest thing that most sophisticated companies can substitute for in a heartbeat.

What they can't ever substitute for is the essence of who a person is, the experience of them, their relationships. If we learn to respect that value, appreciate that honor, then there is no substituting for it, and that's the magic.

Fear Is Not the Answer

A few years ago, I was asked to speak with a new CEO at a large multinational financial services organization. In our first meeting, he asked me, "Do you have a leadership litmus test for me, Carl?"

I could think of at least one. "First," I said, "when your team sees your name on call display, are they excited or afraid?"

Want to guess his response? It wasn't even a response. "Oh, thanks a lot, Carl. You're telling me everyone is afraid of me."

What kind of
leader are you?
How do you know?

I sat back and smiled. "Actually, I just asked a question, Tom. But your interpretation is interesting."

He doubled down, saying, "Well, Carl, maybe this is where we'll agree to disagree."

"How so?"

"I think leveraging fear is a good thing."

And I said, "If you understood how fear incapacitates, you might appreciate otherwise. There is almost always a better alternative. If you needed a pure reaction—like when your toddler is walking toward a moving car that they don't see— a scare tactic would be beneficial. But in the day to day of your business, it would rarely be helpful. Go ahead and leverage it, then ask yourself if you think people on the receiving end, in that moment, want to give you their best."

"Well…" he replied, clearly unconvinced.

"Let me explain," I continued. "When you scare people from time to time, they get the job done. So you walk away feeling reinforced for the approach you took. But I would suggest that their response—or more accurately their reaction—is short-lived. They got it done all right, but only because they had to, and usually only to the extent requested. In other words, fear's effectiveness pales in comparison to inspiring someone to want to give you and the company more of their precious discretionary energy."

"I don't know…" Tom still wasn't convinced.

"Let me put it to you this way. If I were to share a few things that I've heard people say behind the scenes about what they do *not* like about having you as their new CEO, how would you feel?"

Tom perked up, eyes bright, taking on a more aggressive posture. "Like what?"

"Like, and I won't share their names, but I heard…" And then I made something up.

Tom was not pleased.

He said, "I want to know their names. But don't worry, I'll ensure that I address it professionally. I simply want to..." and he carried on with some examples of next steps and his rationalization for addressing the comments.

I said, "I want you to notice your automatic reaction—to find out who they are, to rectify the situation. Well, there are two things I would like you to convince me of. Firstly, when you strike fear into someone, do you think they want to carry on working; and secondly, do you think they feel inspired to keep working for or with you? For example, if I said something to you in public, and you found it disrespectful, inaccurate, clearly not supportive, and even threatening to your ability to make a terrific public impression, how would you respond? Would you still want to put your best effort into addressing the opportunity at hand with me?"

"No, of course not—I'd want to distance myself from you."

"That's right. And most people react this way when they feel threatened. Let's call it 'flight,' which would be particularly prevalent, because the 'fight' option would likely be mitigated for people on your teams by virtue of your seniority."

I added, "Right then, you were triggered. And I want you to know that I made up that story, for your benefit. Notice where you went with it. I know that altruistically you were saying you just wanted to know more so you could fix the problem—but was that the full extent of your intent? Is there any chance you wanted to defend yourself and/or reprimand them in some way? Also notice how, when the seniority is on your side, you might be more inclined to lean in. Let's say, 'fight' is more of an option for you than for others."

"But you were making it up, right?"

I said, "Yes, but my key point relates to your default reaction. Did you immediately start making the comments about you or about them? Were you frustrated with the comments? Or were you inclined to feel compassion for anyone on your team feeling that way, because perhaps there must be some misunderstanding and you don't want anyone to feel like that if you can help it?"

Here is the point: Fear should rarely be the go-to. Rather, "ask and inspire" is the preferred route.

In *Keep Sharp*, Sanjay Gupta writes, "Don't try to inspire people with fear. It doesn't work and it doesn't last... An action that starts in the emotional centers of the brain bypasses the judgment and executive function areas of the brain as well. As a result, the reaction may be intense and immediate, but it is also often uncoordinated and transient... Fear-based messaging will never lead to a long-term effective strategy because it is not the way we are wired."

That same CEO said to me, "I have a question for you. I'm a little bit perplexed by you, because you seem to be so willing to be open and honest with me, brave even, when..." and then he paused.

"Please, finish your thought, Tom."

"When people..." Pause again...

"When people often seem afraid of you?" I offered.

He nodded.

"You need to know," I said, "I'm not afraid of you. Your request for this candid conversation and the honesty with which you are sharing are refreshing and encouraging. You don't have a guard up, and you're sincerely curious about how to become even more effective in this new role.

"From a strategic perspective, I approach discussions like this thinking, What is the absolute worst thing that can happen? You disagree with me. And this is how that plays out. You disagree because you've got some experience that can help me better understand. Awesome, coach me, mentor me, teach me; learning is always a two-way street. But what you can't do, Tom, is agree with me and then do nothing constructive about it, letting habits of old take hold. I think you know that would not serve you, or others, well.

"So, where is the downside? You agree with me, we put it into action. You disagree with me, you teach me, coach me, mentor me. Fantastic. Either way, we learn and benefit together."

And he said, "So, why don't more people approach me like this?"

"Because when you disagree with them, you may do it in a disagreeable way. Which is why I often ask, 'Can you, Leader X, disagree with someone and not be disagreeable?'"

Which is just another way of asking, "What is it like to be in your presence?"

Tom later told me that this single question stuck with him for some time—like a thorn in his side. We had fun and ended up spending a lot more time together as he settled into his role. This conversation had "helped tremendously" (Tom's words), but he wanted to do more with his actions. He became an active student of his own experience—in other words, he became more aware of what it was like to be in his presence.

Did he observe people looking more positively energized after leaving his meetings, or not? He had many examples on both ends of the spectrum. In either case, he consciously noted how his body language, tone of voice, and selection of words drove the results. He found the themes and developed greater consistency for the positive impact he desired to cocreate, and he became more disciplined at practicing what worked and eliminating the approaches that did not.

His improved self-awareness led to enhanced social awareness, and that made all the difference. Before he retired, he
was regarded fondly by most—and to his last day, he felt that,
more than anything, this was his greatest legacy. His love for
others and his desire to see them succeed turned out to be
the secret sauce of his company's remarkable success.

6

Whole Leadership

WAS TALKING to a leader recently; let's call her Samantha. She was about to leave her current firm to become the CEO of another large organization, in her specialty area, and was excited about chairing her first meeting. As she told me about this big opportunity, she asked, "Knowing me, Carl, what would you say I should be thinking about heading into my first meeting with the new team?"

I replied, "How well do you know any of the executives on your new senior leadership team?"

"I think most of them know quite a bit about me," she said.

"But that's not what I asked," I replied. "Knowing *about* someone is quite different from you actually knowing them, as individuals: their hopes, dreams, fears, aspirations, strengths, weaknesses, interests. Do you think this distinction matters? If someone knew these things about you, do you think it would affect their ability to empathize with, relate to, and more effectively team with you?"

"You bet," she said.

"Well, just know that the same is true regarding your ability to empathize with them. After all, how can you empathize with someone you don't know? Situationally perhaps, but not personally. That's where positively affecting a whole person comes into play. It's the whole person who chooses to work with you every day—not some partial facade."

"My gut agrees with you, Carl. But let's be honest, it will take some time for that information to arise during the natural course of things. So, what should I focus on in my upcoming meeting?"

"Before I answer that, I'll just point out that most leaders I know, even after many years of teaming, do not know most of what I just highlighted about the people they team with. But the ones who do develop their relationships consciously and intentionally see the performance of the team flourish as a result. So, I wouldn't leave it to chance that this information will arise during the natural course of things. It will require clear intention and prioritization—your team members either matter to you, as individuals, or they don't. Your actions will tell the tale and your degree of influence will magnify, or not, accordingly."

I said, "So when you walk into that meeting room, what are you planning to focus on?"

"You know, the current state of our industry. The strategy needed moving forward. Making sure everybody is doing what needs to get done. The problems, and how can we solve them."

Everything she said was important. But it was all on a strategic level, not a human level. Samantha was thinking about tasks, not people, except to ask them, "Where are you on this? What are the updates?"

That's a typical meeting—everyone reports in, and then they leave. That's it.

I said to Samantha, "So, what will you do in your first *few* meetings? How will you contribute to what you called your problem-solving process? Other than administering?"

As expected, she didn't like that. I had chosen that word—"administration"—on purpose. In the educational system, administration is top of the leadership house. In politics too, leaders "administer" government. But in the business world, senior levels of responsibility are described as "management" or "leadership."

So, I added, "Let's explore some language and see if it makes a difference. In your new organization, are you being paid top dollar to administer, manage, or lead?"

Samantha replied, "I'm not sure I understand the question."

I smiled. "If our leaders can't distinguish between administering, managing, and leading, how much leading are they doing? For fun, I'll suggest that most leaders manage; they don't lead. What do you think about that?"

Samantha smiled in return and said, "You just helped me recall an earlier conversation we had about the three *e*'s of leadership: energize, equip, and empower. So, I suppose you're suggesting that it would be helpful if I thought about how I'll do each of these?"

"That sounds like a great plan. And to encourage you, let me also point out that many senior leaders I have worked with cannot honestly tell me with any level of conscious competence, 'Here is how I attempt to energize' or 'Here is my deliberate method, my process of equipping, my way of empowering my team members.' They don't have any conscious or practiced insights where these three *e*'s are concerned."

"That is encouraging. Thanks, Carl. Any thoughts about where to start?"

"Well, early on, your focus will likely be on how to energize the team and on clarifying what empowerment looks like. And as relationships develop, knowing how to best equip for specific needs will become more apparent. After all, how can you energize, empower, or equip people you don't really know? If their respective strengths and weaknesses are still unknown to you, how can you align them to complement one another and to optimize the quality of the team's influence? If, as leaders, we want to positively influence others in a chosen, purposeful direction, we need to prioritize *knowing* them first—something very few make the time to do. It won't just happen naturally. The most effective ninety-day plan starts with a focus on getting to know one another as people, not just as widgets in respective roles."

I then reminded Samantha about another favorite source of hers, Simon Sinek. Sinek often emphasizes that leaders are responsible for the people, who are responsible for the people, who are responsible for the people, who service the market. And if you don't understand that, then you're not leading. Sinek and I speak the same language, and I've enjoyed diving deeper into the relevance of our biology, because biology cuts through a lot of the politics and allows us to automatically think in human terms, focusing on our common humanity. The point being that having responsibility for other people implies you know them well enough to lead and influence them effectively under varying circumstances.

Samantha, having an undergraduate degree in biology, asked if I had any final insights where our biology was concerned, a subject we often enjoyed exploring together.

I said, "Because we've all evolved as a species, we share some undeniable biological features." I then elaborated on some of what I've already shared. "If, for instance, you perceive anything that I do or say as a threat, as soon as you feel threatened, your biochemistry changes, and as a result, you cannot access some of the best of your intellect. That's not a maybe. So, when people say, 'But not everyone reacts in the same way'—OK, true. But once you're triggered, physiological and biological cues take over. Thinking in terms of biology allows us to view things more objectively. If someone behaves defensively, it's because they're feeling threatened. Are you the source of that threat? And what can you do to support them in that state?"

Samantha shared, "I can see how challenging and yet inspiring that can be—the opportunity to affect others in a way that helps them feel safe and connected and allows them to grow beyond levels that they thought possible. Carl, one last question: Do you think that, biologically speaking, we crave empathy from others?"

"To be seen, heard, understood, and appreciated—to matter—does that sound relevant to you?"

Samantha nodded.

"We're literally hardwired to be loving creatures. If we didn't know how to collaborate and cooperate, we wouldn't exist. We're a relatively weak species. It takes us a year to learn how to walk, and longer to talk, and if we were literally on our own, survival of the fittest, we'd all be extinct. Our ability to collaborate and cooperate allowed us to evolve. It's as simple as that."

I continued with some additional thoughts that hopefully sound familiar to you now. "But what makes us want to collaborate and cooperate, and how do we do that in an optimal way? Well, science shows us that when we respond with loving intent—even pausing long enough to ask ourselves what that would look like before we respond—our emotional center and our thinking center function more harmoniously. Which makes sense. If there's no threat on the horizon, I'm simply focused on 'What can I do to make this moment better?' When we arc toward the loving end of the spectrum,

What is it like to be in your presence? Is your practice one of creating new, helpful possibilities or of constant objection and difficulty?

we optimize our biological and biochemical ability to access the best of our intellect. I can be generous. Whether I need a memory or access to thought leadership, whatever it may be, the safer I feel, the more comfortable and supported I feel, the more capable I am of accessing the best of what I know."

"Thanks, Carl. I'll make a mantra out of 'I want to access the best of my intellect.' Because, let's face it, the business world is always saying that all it cares about is what we think. It doesn't care about what or how we feel. But how interesting, because, as you point out, how I feel informs whether I can give you the best of my thoughts. I get it. Effective leadership creates a safe, empowering environment, so everyone can access the best of their intellects. For me to ensure I'm leading and not just managing, I'll bring an intentional focus to the three *e*'s, while adding a fourth, exemplar. As you've often said to me, if I'm not modeling the very thing that I'm discussing, then others simply won't believe me. And we need to believe in one another if we're going to optimize how we work as a team. Is that a fair assessment?"

"To have a senior leader, with your level of formal authority, go out of their way to make time to listen to me, to know me, to understand me, to help me, to challenge me, to support me—I can't think of a better place to start. Your new team is lucky to have this ever-evolving leader who brings intention to leadership itself, and who intuitively understands that it starts with walking the talk.

"Many think that leadership is about telling others what to do. Their focus is almost entirely on others. But the most effective leaders understand that it starts within themselves. As their self-awareness elevates, they become more proficient at self-regulation, management, and leadership. Not only does this facilitate a greater ability to empathize with others, but it's the key to optimal influence. This is whole leadership."

What It's Like to Be in Your Presence

Leadership is about how we influence ourselves and, in turn, how we influence others. Leaders often overlook the leading ourselves part, and yet, as the illustration below shows, leading ourselves is foundational. Our own experience will have taught us that if we do not do for ourselves what we hope to influence within others, our impact will be limited. In other words, there will be few voluntary followers to be found. After all, the most basic definition of a leader is one who has voluntary followers. No followers, no leader.

WHOLE LEADERSHIP

STRENGTHEN
COMPANY

LEAD OTHERS

LEAD SELF

STRENGTHEN COMPANY	LEAD OTHERS	LEAD SELF
Role model alignment with mission	Inspire, develop, and champion others	Improve self-awareness and optimize energy
Guide with values and ethics	Infuse others with positive energy	Self-manage effectively
Make the entire company better	Participate in and build a strong team	Act positively and steadily under pressure
		Stay open-minded and flexible
		Learn constantly

Positively influencing others begins with how effectively we lead ourselves. And since we cannot consciously change what we are not aware of, self-awareness is a logical starting point. The more aware I am of my physical, emotional, and mental states, the greater my ability to affect them constructively and positively.

Think back to Henry in chapter 1. He admitted right away that he was not conscious of the energy he brought into the room. He wasn't aware of the effect he was having on others—*of what it was like to be in his presence*. And that started with Henry himself.

When Henry walked into that meeting with Lisa and me, what state was he in? Was he angry, joyful, stressed, tired? Or maybe just distracted, thinking about a report he had to finish for Friday? Whatever he was feeling or thinking surely affected how he showed up—but Henry hadn't given it a moment's thought. He was thinking about Friday's report.

If you're thinking about a moment that just passed, or one still to come, then by definition you're not present in this moment. Your audience will always sense this. "I suppose I'm not important enough to capture your attention." Which will make them wonder why; distraction begets more distraction. Which is not great for the focus, opportunities, or possibilities that could have otherwise emerged.

During a talk I attended in January 2021 called "The Neuroscience of Change," professor and author Daniel Siegel shared:

> The mind is not a synonym for brain activity. Well, it's partly brain activity, but it's something more. The self is much broader than the brain. It's much bigger in many ways than even the body. Our identity as human beings is very much related to characteristics that place us in a field of belonging. That's one of the most important things, so when we discuss the neuroscience of change, we want to understand, how

does the self change? How does identity change? How does belonging change over time? You could say there are many facets of the mind, but whatever one you're referring to, it's an emergent aspect of energy flow.

I asked Henry, "How conscious were you of the energy you brought into this room?" Leadership is all about energy. Effective leaders manifest what's possible (to the benefit of themselves and others) by inspiring meaningful action—within themselves and others. In Siegel's book *Aware: The Science and Practice of Presence*, he shares a time when he was invited to participate in a weeklong gathering of 150 scientists, many of them physicists and mathematicians, where his primary curiosity revolved around the question "What is energy?" Ultimately several would say, as Siegel writes in *Aware*:

> In one way or another, *energy is the movement from possibility to actuality.* That's it.
> Say what?
> Energy is the movement from a *potential* to *that potential being realized.* That's what they mean by the basic statement that energy is the movement from possibility to actuality. Energy is the actualization of possibility.

So, how can our biology increase the odds that we will optimize our performance while more consistently actualizing our potential? Siegel also shares that "regular practice supports the movement from a state created during a practice to a trait that becomes a learned skill or way of being. A trait essentially is a baseline propensity or way of behaving that happens without effort or conscious planning in a person's life. What you create in the moment can become strengthened in the long run with practice. This is how a state becomes a trait." Since most of our daily choices arise from our subconscious (autopilot), ensuring that we're programming a healthy subconscious through disciplined practice is crucial.

The bridge from theory to mastery is, therefore, practice. Since we, as individual humans who are being, represent pure potentiality, the living embodiment of possibility, we can circle back to our fundamental questions: What is it like to be in your presence? Uplifting with possibility or deflating with impossibility? Do you (and others) see you as the radiant possibility you are, or as a problem? Is your practice one of creating new, helpful possibilities or of constant objection and difficulty? Do you find it helpful to consider that we don't have a life, we are life—a unique manifestation of life itself, an amalgam of experience (and possibility), never to be again? The very essence of which is our animating life force, our life energy?

With this in mind, what practical guidance can you access to optimize the quality, focus, and expression of your life force—your energy—and your resulting influence?

Why do I ask this? Because to be at your best (to the benefit of all involved), it will help to have a deeper understanding of how to improve the quality, focus, and expression of your energy. If you don't do this intentionally, then how can you expect any level of improvement to last? Without awareness and consistent practice, you will experience states that rise and fall from time to time, with little or no chance of becoming aspirational traits.

How can you self-manage and improve these three domains: the quality, focus, and expression of your energy? First, it helps to be aware of what each entail, at a high level. Then you can have some fun tailoring next steps to improve in each area.

PART II

BIOLOGY SUGGESTS THAT THE QUALITY, FOCUS, AND EXPRESSION OF YOUR ENERGY MATTERS

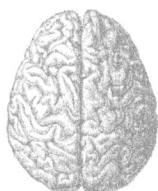

7

The Quality
of Your Energy

T O UNDERSTAND the quality of your energy, it can be helpful to think about it across three states: physical, emotional, and mental. These three states affect your ability to be resilient in the face of challenges. Practice the fundamentals within each state and you can migrate from fragile to resilient to anti-fragile, and from states to traits.

We often hear about the importance of character (implying "character traits"), but character doesn't just magically appear; it's cultivated, demonstrated, lived, and reflected in every word and action. Not surprisingly, what it's like to be in your presence will be nicely connected to the cultivated content of your character.

This all starts with your physical state—mindfully (and intentionally) controlling the controllable: getting quality sleep, eating well, and keeping active. I won't go into great detail here because there are countless books on each of these topics, but I will share a few highlights.

As part of my Heroic coaching certification journey, we dove deeply into the fundamentals, starting with sleep—

the many benefits of which you can look into at great length, if interested. Quick rule of thumb: Anything that can reduce your body temperature before you go to bed will help you fall asleep, such as ensuring you don't eat anything within three hours of bedtime or not exercising within three hours of your head hitting the pillow. Keeping a cooler room will help too, as will reducing screen time and shutting down your focused attention (in other words, work) at least one hour before bed. From a biological standpoint, increasing your levels of melatonin (the primary sleep hormone) and reducing cortisol (a primary stress hormone) will enhance your ability to fall asleep. That's why avoiding screens, which emit the blue light that keeps cortisol levels high while suppressing melatonin, will help.

Just think, we haven't had electricity all that long. Our bodies used to be well attuned to feeling sleepy as soon as the sun set. Now, with so many screens and other sources of artificial light, unless we proactively, more consciously manage our exposure, our bodies won't know it's time to sleep. There are also suggestions that as little as five minutes of meditation in the morning can help us fall asleep fifteen minutes faster in the evening.

Of course, you do not have to believe all this without question. You can experiment, practice, and observe for yourself.

With respect to nutrition, you don't need me to tell you how or what to ingest. Idiosyncratically, see what fuel works best within you and plan (over time) to leave out what does not. Experience has taught me one very effective tip that has had the biggest impact over the shortest period of time and can be realized by executing on one key principle: Don't drink your sugar. This one thought, operationalized, has helped many a friend, as their water intake went up and their juice, pop, and alcohol consumption went down.

Regarding movement, we were born to move. Many moons ago, we put our movement to good (and essential) use hunting and gathering. Of course, our eight hours a day (or three thousand minutes a week) of movement have given way to convenience everywhere we look. For most of us, finding the next meal does not prove as strenuous as it once did, nor preparing it, nor cleaning up afterward. I've heard it said that, in terms of its impact on our overall health and well-being, our relatively sedentary lifestyle is the new smoking. In Katy Bowman's book *Movement Matters*, she shares that "Movement, just like the cell wall, the mitochondria, the cytoskeleton, and the nucleus, is a part of every working cell. Cells don't work without movement, and you aren't fully operational without all of your cells working well. The movement of a part today is what affords it the ability to move tomorrow."

Are you moving throughout your day? Are you targeting a certain number of steps, stretching every so often, scheduling meetings that do not last more than ninety minutes before ensuring movement, et cetera? Again, experiment and see what leads to the best version of you being available, while also observing the habits of those around you and encouraging more of what's working for them too.

When these ideas, or the many that I'm sure you've discovered for yourself, are consistently practiced, your physical state is optimized. The fine-tuning never ends, and needs can change over time, but you get the idea. When we've just enjoyed a wonderful sleep, our last meal is agreeing with us, and we've been moving consistently, how do you think this fine physical state affects our emotional state? Or its opposite: Imagine a terrible night's sleep, your last meal is still upsetting your stomach, and you've been chained to your desk for a week... How's your emotional state? The former leads to a sense of openness and contentment where patience, empathy, compassion, and encouragement are likely to follow. The latter leaves you feeling like your fuse is short, your attention span narrowed, and your mind prone to more selfish, survival tendencies.

In a state where our self-awareness is compromised, we often feel like a victim and are in no position to want to self-regulate, focus, or lead for the benefit of all involved. In this state, unconscious biases will easily arise and often lead to less than desirable choices. If you're feeling insecure or threatened, might you want to socialize only with those who are likely to agree with your point of view? Say hello to confirmation bias.

We're hearing more and more about the mental health challenges experienced by so many. What we don't hear much about is how our physical and emotional states can act as precursors to a healthier mental state. Physiology can also drive psychology, an understanding not widely discussed. In his book *Keep Sharp*, after discussing the physical benefits of exercise, Sanjay Gupta points out:

> There are generally two ways that exercise benefits the brain. For one, exercise effectively uses circulating blood sugar and reduces inflammation while stimulating the release of growth factors, substances that promote both the proliferation and function of cells. In the brain, these growth factors support the health of new neurons, the recruitment of blood vessels, and the survival of all neurons. The other way that exercise can benefit the brain may seem a little less objective, but it is no less important. We now know that regular movement measurably reduces stress and anxiety while improving sleep and mood—all of which can also positively affect brain structure and function. These combined effects

build critically important brain resilience in the long term and help pave the way for us to be creative and insightful and to solve problems in the short term.

Developing and delivering on the fundamentals optimize our physical state, which positively affects our biochemical and emotional states, both of which then optimize our perspective, ability to stay intentional, and willingness to practice new and improved ways of approaching challenges. Continue practicing and notice how your states become your aspirational traits over time.

Safety Allows Us to Grow and Blossom

When our physical state is primed for energized tranquility, our emotional state will arc toward a loving response for what comes our way. Sustained with self-awareness of our triggers, coping mechanisms in hand, and focused on servicing a win-win (being mindful of what we want versus what we don't want), we set ourselves up for a possibility-charged mental state—one where we are primed for choosing words and actions that align with the best of our imagination and creativity. Focused forward, growth-oriented, and more agile, we continually improve our ability to positively impact ourselves and others.

When Google did Project Aristotle, its research project around the attributes every team needs to access peak performance, the number one quality was psychological safety. In *Your Body Is Your Brain*, Amanda Blake writes that our brain "evolved to optimize access to safety (brainstem), connection (limbic area), and social status, or what we might refer to as dignity or respect (cerebral cortex). Just as plants take physical shape in response to the availability of sunlight, soil, and water, the human brain evolved to take shape in response to the availability of these three essential 'nutrients.'"

And how can we access safety? By ensuring we feel safe physically, emotionally, and then, yes, psychologically. People need to feel safe so they can take risks and be vulnerable in front of their colleagues. And since we feel before we think, our emotional state will impact our mental state.

How are you feeling? How is that informing your thoughts? How are your feelings and thoughts informing your words and actions? How are your feelings and thoughts and words and actions informing the experience I just had of working with you (and you with me)?

You can work on this. You can practice it, in that sequence. You can see when somebody you're working with is numb, excited, bored, interested, curious.

Now the question is, what do you do about it?

Inspiring Others by "Breathing Life" into Them

Do you champion those in your care? Do you know that your every word and action either helps them move in a desired direction or further away from it? To inspire another is to "breathe life" into them. The leader in you becomes an expert in this regard, knowing that your behavior toward another will reflect how effectively you lead yourself. What is your self-talk like? Do the words you focus on move you in your desired direction? Since a significant percentage of your communication is with yourself, a tremendous benefit accrues if you practice being mindful of the words you choose.

Your physical and emotional states can act as precursors to a healthier mental state.

Would you say the quality of your physical and emotional state impacts the quality of your inner dialogue? My guess is that when you consistently honor your fundamentals (sleep, nutrition, movement), you tend toward a "bring it on" way of talking with yourself. And if your fundamentals are regularly compromised, you risk an inner dialogue that sounds more like "I'm just no good." Can you see how, depending upon your answers, your influence on others can be dramatically affected? Being more aware, honest, and kind with yourself can help you get it right more often than not. Practice makes progress, allowing you to close the gap between your current impact and that of your most effective self.

So, the quality of your energy matters. Thinking back to Henry, after he and I explored the concepts shared above, he told me how, on the morning of our meeting, he had slept poorly after working late the night before, skipped breakfast, missed his workout for the ninth day in a row... No wonder I encountered a less than optimal version of him. He closed the gap between that and his optimal version first by becoming more aware of the issue, and then by mapping some easy wins to improve his physical and emotional state.

How conscious are you of the quality of your energy? How about those in your care? Do you see how their physical and emotional states impact their mental state?

Burning the Candle at Both Ends

At a lunch meeting, an executive used the expression "burning the candle at both ends." I thought it might be fun to ask, "Metaphorically speaking, what happens when you do burn a candle at both ends? In all seriousness, what's the visual?"

He laughed and said, "Well, if nothing else, eventually, there's no more wax."

I said, "Exactly right. The wax is energy, stored energy. When you constantly give, there comes a time when there's nothing left. And you can't give what you don't have. Just like that candle, when the energy is depleted, the light—that is you—can no longer burn brightly."

He replied, "That's such a simple visual. I guess you're telling me that I'm only kidding myself if I keep pretending that I don't need sleep or I don't need good nutrition or I don't need to exercise and move throughout my day."

I said, "Bingo."

He shared that he feels like his company is attempting to robotize people.

I said, "Well, I'm sure you won't be surprised to hear that you're not robots. You're burning the candle at both ends, pretending like you're going to be just fine. But you're not—you won't be as lucid, clear-headed, thoughtful, creative, imaginative, patient, and so on. Not to mention what you will be doing to your overall state of health and well-being."

Although it's easy to speak about being positive, steady under pressure, open-minded, and flexible, if you compromise or ignore the quality of your energy, these other desirable leadership qualities will elude you. If instead you focus on continual learning, you can harness the benefits that come with practicing being a student of your own experience. As you experiment with what works best for you, your improvement will translate as a more desirable, positive impact on others.

And now you are positioned nicely to lead others (the next level in the whole leadership pyramid on page 80). As a radiant exemplar, the quality of your energy will attract others to want more of the same within themselves. Not overnight, but rather over a lifetime. This is the impetus that encourages others to follow you. We all start at different places, for any number of reasons. Those reasons will forever remain a part of our past, so now we focus on this moment (which, in turn, will dictate the quality of our future moments). It's all about progress, not perfection.

Lessons from Sport

At one point in my career, I was asked to take on a national coaching role in which I had leadership responsibility pertaining to a wonderful faculty of external professional coaches. This led to my being asked to facilitate several charitable events involving Olympic athletes. In addition to enjoying the relationships that evolved, I met with a number of top athletes and their coaches.

The exposure and shared learnings were terrific. Something mentioned more than once was how many athletes knew not to make key decisions if they were either hungry, angry, lonely, or tired (HALT). The athletes were more aware than most of the bridge between mindset, perspective, and perception and the body. Not surprising when you consider they represent the best of the best when it comes to peak physical performance.

Let's unpack this a little. Hungry. Do you think Olympic athletes care about their nutrition? You bet. What about anger? Do you think they are mindful of their emotional state and how it relates to maintaining peak performance levels? Yes again. If you've ever witnessed an Olympic Games, you may have felt there were as many coaches as athletes in attendance. How about loneliness? Have you ever heard a gold medalist being interviewed about their accomplishment and when asked if they would like to thank anyone, respond with "Nope, it was all me"? They are well aware that no one succeeds as an island; it takes a village to win gold. Lastly, tired. Do you think athletes care about the quality of their sleep? Practically goes without saying.

Do you realize that, within your organization, you're the corporate equivalent of these athletes? You too have incredible mounting external pressure that always requires you do more with less and achieve peak levels of performance, despite the outside pressures.

How much do you respect the rules of HALT? Are you mindful about what you eat, and do you appreciate its impact on your performance? How about your level of emotional self-awareness? (Hopefully, this part is developing nicely following our ongoing conversation.) Feel lonely? It's OK to need help. And tired—maybe we can skip that one—I'm sure you always prioritize a great night's sleep and always feel invigorated in the morning. (Said with sarcasm, to be clear!) You might do well to pay attention to these areas if you want to improve your well-being and performance. Plan your work accordingly and then work your plan.

Neurons that fire together wire together, and our repeated choices impact our wiring. So, let's be respectful of this fact as we endeavor to increase our self-awareness, make conscious choices, and reinforce our default (autopilot) thinking patterns. And never lose hope. Neuroplasticity allows our hardwiring to change. Every new attempt inherently carries within it hope!

Another tip I picked up from athletes: The body responds the same way to an emotionally charged memory or projection as it does to an experience of the same thing. The point? Visualize what you want, not what you don't want, and picture doing all the best things to get there. It is about the journey and not the destination, even when visualizing. And when things do not go the way you planned or hoped, experiment with replaying the occurrence in your mind's eye, but this time making an optimal choice that produces the desired outcome. This anchors the learning and better prepares you in the event that a similar situation comes your way again. You can even imagine how you would feel when your envisioned future comes to pass. And practice feeling that way as if it had indeed come to pass already. When you practice holding these thoughts and feelings in the present moment, you may find that life conspires accordingly for your benefit.

8

The Focus
of Your Energy

O UR RECEPTIONIST, let's call her Susan, had been at
the same organization as me for years and knew everyone there. She was the first face that everyone would
see. One day she asked me if I could give her some advice.

"Carl, I've got a quiet moment with no one coming in,"
she said. "I'm sorry to call you away from your office but I
wonder if there is something I can do to address how down
I'm feeling. I'm just really struggling," she added. "Do you
have a quick hit for me—perhaps a suggestion or point of
view that helps those who are experiencing a difficult time?"

I smiled and said, "Well, one quick hit might be to recall
that the easiest way to get out of your own head is to put
yourself in the service of someone else. So, may I remind
you, lovingly, that you are the first wonderful face that everyone sees when they walk out of the elevators? And there is
literally no one in this organization, regardless of rank or
experience, who has the initial influence that you do, the
very second that someone walks in. I'm curious: have you
ever realized that, ever played with that?"

She replied, "No, I never thought about it that way before. In fact, I've tended to diminish the importance of my role relative to all the highly educated professionals we work with every day. Although, I will say I've observed that you seem to try to positively influence others, every day, which is probably why I'm so comfortable asking you for help."

"That's very kind of you to say, Susan, thank you. I'm sure we all do this at times. The challenge is in how to consistently affect others, consciously and positively. I'd like to think that everyone can appreciate the power of this practice," I said. "All to say, it's your choice to make. So, what I'd like you to do, just for fun, is with the next ten people who enter this space, practice being more conscious of the quality of the experience you are cocreating with them and for them."

"Can you give me a couple of examples of what I might expect?"

"Sure. Maybe someone's coming in for an interview and you can put them at ease, because you know the personalities of the people they are going to meet. Maybe it's someone who's bringing in the latest coffee supply for the lunchroom and who makes so many deliveries that they are not accustomed to being treated with overt respect. And you can honor them by telling them how much we're enjoying that particular coffee, and we notice that they are always on time, and that means something. I'm going to stop there, because I don't want my examples to become prescriptive; I want it to come from you, as you, in service of the moment. And then at the end of the day—should you feel so inspired—take five minutes before you head home, give me a call, and let me know how it went and if you found anything interesting you'd like to share."

Susan did just that, and when she called, I could hear excitement in her voice. "Oh my gosh, Carl, all of my internal problems seemed to disappear, at least during those moments! I got people smiling. I got them talking and telling stories. It was amazing. A great day. I'm guessing you're not surprised?"

I said, "Here's one thought to ponder: When you find things tough, the odds are that you are focused almost entirely on yourself. The moment you shift your focus to anything outside yourself, in service of the moment, and whoever shares that moment with you, you'll find that you 'get out of your own way,' or 'get out of your own head.' Then you truly let your energy and actions fill the moment and in so doing, remind yourself of your purpose and what you're capable of. Some might call this 'flow' or being 'in the zone.' In the book *Aware*, my friend Daniel Siegel puts it this way: 'Where attention goes, neural firing flows, and neural connection grows.' Bottom line: We can't be a victim if we're not focused on ourselves."

Susan said, "Wow. Isn't that wonderful! This morning, I was being pretty hard on myself. I was down. I was saying to myself, 'I'm a receptionist, what good am I?' I don't know why I was thinking that. I was just feeling sorry for myself."

"Did that shift?" I asked.

"So substantially," she replied, "because I realized that I had an important role to play and could choose to be a good influence on all these people."

Most of us have been conditioned to set static goals: aspiring to this income level, that title, or that office. But a shift occurs when you experiment with dynamic goals, such as "Can I make a habit out of positively affecting the moment, the people within my circle of influence, or the outcome?" Rather than being attached to a static goal (and thereby often feeling down, should the path to it become delayed), you infuse the moment with the best of who you are, contributing in your

unique way, in the hopes of bringing to it a little more progress, joy, and compassion than otherwise might have been.
This sheds some light on the meaning of the old adage that
life really is about the journey, and not just the destination.

In the weeks that followed, Susan put her hand up and
became the office leader for one of the company's sports
teams. She was our captain. She not only recruited people to
the team, but she scheduled the games and the after-parties.
She became a key leader in the office. On the field she was
the leader too, and she was the constant source of support on
the sidelines, as well as being the manager—the foundation
of the team itself. And all because she had become wonderfully, beautifully, positively committed to contributing in a
meaningful way, despite her initial thoughts that her formal
position was perhaps insignificant. How wonderful it was to
observe her willingness to experiment, show up, and focus
her attention—and change the energy of the entire office in
the process. Talk about a multiplier effect. Many senior leaders, those appointed to their positions of privilege and formal
authority, often *speak* about the need to create a positive ripple effect. Susan did it!

ATTITUDE/ENERGY MODEL

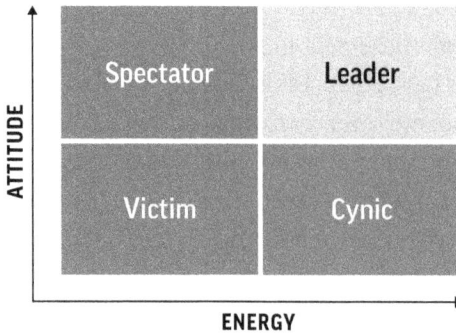

Everything changed for her when she started to consistently ask herself, "What would the leader in me do or say?" As opposed to listening to an inner victim, who used to suggest that life was conspiring against her. I celebrated her amazing leadership and positive impact every chance I could and pointed out that her experience exemplified how life rewards action and how, as my mother taught me, it's wonderfully liberating to practice living into the answers.

As reflected in Susan's story, the next step in becoming the leader you want to be is to examine the focus of your energy. It bears repeating why this is relevant from a biological standpoint. Recall Daniel Siegel reminding us that neural connection grows where our attention goes. Quite literally, what we focus on grows. So, what are you focusing on? Do you set your mind in a way that works for you and others, or against you (or them)? In *Keep Sharp*, Sanjay Gupta quotes a leading pioneer in brain plasticity research, Michael Merzenich, who says, "The patterns of activity of neurons in sensory areas can be altered by patterns of attention. Experience coupled with attention leads to physical changes in the structure and future functioning of the nervous system. This leaves us with a clear physiological fact... moment by moment we choose and sculpt how our ever-changed minds will work. We choose who we will be in the next moment in a very real sense, and these choices are left embossed in physical form in our material selves."

These types of scientific insights compelled me to continue my exploration of what it means to be more intentional about attention. To that end, I encountered two different models that were introduced to me many years ago, in separate moments, but I've seen how effectively they can work together.

Let's start with the Attitude/Energy model on page 102 regarding how we set our minds (our mindset). Claude Lineberry developed it in the 1980s to explain individual motivation based on a person's attitude and the energy they were willing to invest in any given moment. It illustrates how our attitude and energy will affect whether the *leader* in us is present and accounted for or whether the *spectator*, *victim*, or *cynic* are in control.

How does it work? Each quadrant represents a particular mindset, a lens through which we can view the world and interpret data. I like to say that our mindset determines our mindsight: how we see and likely respond to the world around us. Of course, our minds can bounce around from one quadrant to the next depending on the situation and on our conscious practice of staying mindful of our attitude and energy, from moment to moment.

In moments when we have a terrific attitude—loving, constructive, supportive, hopeful, optimistic, you get the picture—but are not very present, our energy is on the lower end of the engagement spectrum, the spectator in us is at the wheel. Think of times when you were actually spectating, like at a sports event, and recall how sometimes you were focused on the game, but many times you were not. Alternatively, if we have plenty of energy to give but our attitude is less than constructive, that's the cynic in us—the "my way or the highway" mentality. And finally, if we don't have a constructive, supportive attitude and are not engaged, that's the victim in us. Hopefully, it's clear that the optimal mindset is the one where we are mindful of cultivating an attitude that represents the more positive end of the spectrum, coupled with a higher energy/presence to match—that's the leader to the fore.

I have found that as soon as I introduce this concept to someone, they become more aware of their current attitude and energy level, thus beckoning the leader in them to come forward. So, you may be wondering why anyone would choose anything other than the leader quadrant. And how can we migrate to the leader mindset if and when we find ourselves in one of the others?

Both great questions. Starting with the first, choosing any of these mindsets has a payoff—otherwise we would never choose them. In brief, as a spectator, we stay safe, out of the game, not exposed, comfortable. We can judge from afar with no direct consequence. On the opposite side, as a cynic, we protect our position, become a right-fighter, our way or the highway. The payoff is we're always right (of course), so we actively defend against another's point of view if it differs from our own. Interestingly, while they're opposites, both the spectator and the cynic allow us a sense of safety regarding our own point of view. But in a professional sense, why would we ever choose the mindset of a victim (in other words, "Woe is me, everything happens to me, look how difficult and unfair this is, look how they made me feel...")? Because as a victim we don't have to do anything. Complaining or criticizing is easier, and we can wallow in our sorrow without acting.

But the leader in us doesn't just observe, or defend for the sake of protecting our ego, or lean into self-pity or inaction. No, the leader is mindful of maintaining a high quality of energy and an attitude that keeps us in the game, of bringing a sense of duty to give our best because it's ours to give, in service of something that matters.

As for the biological relevance of wanting to serve others, Amy Cuddy says it nicely in her bestseller *Presence*: "The link between anxiety and self-absorption is bidirectional; they

You can use your senses to ground yourself in this moment, a fun way to develop the quality of space between stimulus and response.

cause each other. In a review of more than two hundred studies, researchers concluded that the more self-focused we are, the more anxious—and also the more depressed and generally negative—we become."

How to Get the Leader in You to Step Up

So, how do you migrate from any one of these suboptimal mindsets to the leader within? To migrate from the spectator to the leader requires candor and courage. Candor, the quality of being open and honest with oneself and others, is easiest to access when we remember that we are a one-of-a-kind original, a unique amalgam of experience never to be again. Remembering this can help us stay true to who we are, the feelings and thoughts we have, and the choice we can make to share proactively and constructively if we think there may be some benefit in doing so.

If this is new to you, then courage is the help you need. It does take courage to act in the face of uncertainty, but the leader in you is up to it. Elaine Welteroth (an instructor of the Masterclass online education series) says that before we speak, we can THINK: If what we're about to say is true, helpful, inspiring, necessary, and kind, then not only can we speak up but we must. Deepak Chopra shared a similar tool, emphasizing truth, necessity, and kindness. When you have all five (or at least three) of these criteria, then experience (and research) would prompt you to speak up.

One further tip derives from the origin of the word "courage" itself: "heart in action." If your heart is guiding you to speak up in service of the moment, then a practice of trusting it will lead to more and more courage. *You* may not agree with this, but the leader in you surely will. If you are motivated by love and guided by reason, you are likely on the right path. I would add that without an appreciation of the loving side of the equation, you'll have limited access to your reason.

If I find myself looking at the situation as a cynic, how do I shift so that the leader in me is present? Well, do you know the answer to every question ever asked? Me neither. So why do we place so much pressure on ourselves to pretend we do? The key to migrating from cynic to leader is curiosity. If we practice keeping an open mind and focus on collective learning, then we'll migrate quite easily. This goes hand in hand with one of my favorite coaching questions: "How do you know?" Whenever someone seems sure (about anything), it can be informative to inquire accordingly. This way, we can determine if their opinion is based on clear facts or something else, perhaps speculation.

As for those times when you choose to see things through the lens of a victim, observe how much attention you're placing on yourself, as opposed to the contribution you can make to the moment (in service of both you and those in your care). As Susan the receptionist discovered, choosing the victim mindset when you're focused on helping others is difficult. The leader in you orients yourself around this: service.

The optimal lens is the leader mindset. Checking in with yourself, at any moment, regarding your current attitude and degree of presence will keep the leader in you available. "Am I practicing gratitude and placing my attention upon what I can do to make this moment just a little better than it would have been in my absence?" This is what the leader in you does, habitually. When you ask, "What would the leader in me do or say next?" you will get markedly different results than if you asked how the cynic might react. In *Man's Search for Meaning*, Viktor Frankl writes, "Between stimulus and response there is a space. In that space is our power to choose our response. In our response lies our growth and our freedom." How we set our minds will impact our choices, because how we see the issue *is* the issue. The spectator, victim, cynic, and leader will interpret events differently and that will dramatically impact their responses—which may range from inspiring and proactive to unconscious and defensive. Susan was feeling like a victim. Then she consciously shifted into a leader mindset—and became an entirely different influencer (and leader) as a result.

Our mindset will determine the quality of our mindsight (how we see the issue). The leader within can choose to live our core values and ensure all decisions align with our mission or purpose. This is how the Attitude/Energy model complements the second one, the Intention–Action–Impact model. So, let's discuss that next.

Putting Intentions into Action

The bridge from intention to impact is our actions (including the words that accompany them). I have no doubt that most of us feel that we are well-intentioned. We did not wake up this morning thinking, "I can't wait to get into work so that I can derail everyone's day!" I also suspect that most of us want to optimize and maximize the quality of our impact. So, why do we sometimes fall short?

Becoming more mindful of our words and actions can help—particularly if we proactively consider what we want to be intentional about. Do you know your top five personal values or virtues? (More on these in chapter 15.) Do you practice filtering your words and actions through them? Many do not, but the consistently highest-performing version of yourself will. If kindness is a top value, then pause (as Viktor Frankl suggested, between any stimulus and a given response) and adapt your choices to ensure you convey kindness. As a repeated practice, this grooves the neural pathways in your brain to make it a default competence over time. In other words, you reprogram your autopilot.

INTENTION-ACTION-IMPACT MODEL

Intention   Action   Impact

To be clear, the leader in you more often than not will practice being intentional about your attention. The leader knows your top values (and those of your organization or team) and ensures that you choose words and actions that consciously align. If you're well-intentioned most of the time, and interested in optimizing your impact, then what gets in the way? Research conducted by the Institute for Health and Human Potential suggests that five things more than anything else tend to pull us away from our conscious best:

1. When someone speaks to us in a condescending way

2. When we perceive a lack of support

3. When we perceive an ask to be unreasonable

4. When we perceive something as unfair

5. When we're never asked for our point of view (in other words, not given a voice)

Having shared this many times, I know that most of us can relate to how these slights can sting. But are you ever the cause of any of these? The leader in you will do your part to ensure the answer is no. Put another way, are you mindful of your words and their resulting impact? How do you evidence your support for others? How do you ensure others perceive the asks of them as reasonable and fair? And do you make a point of asking others for their thoughts while creating a safe space for them to share their voice?

If we are none the wiser, every one of these five triggers play on our emotions. That's why being more intelligent about our emotions is so important. And I have seen two more ways in which this Intention–Action–Impact model proves helpful.

Firstly, did you know that we tend to assess our own performance based on our intentions, but the rest of the world evaluates us based on our impact? All the more reason to ensure that we become more conscious of what we want to be intentional about *and* to ensure that our words and actions align accordingly.

Secondly, when on the receiving end of an experience that we dislike, most of us (perhaps unconsciously) assume ill intent on the part of the other person. Know this and pay attention next time. How would you respond if instead of assuming the worst you gave them the benefit of the doubt? What if you knew they were well-intentioned but they simply chose their words or actions without much thought? Intention matters. It doesn't take away our responsibility for the impact we cocreate, but it at least provides context that can allow us to stay focused instead of distracted and defensive.

Mindfulness

Susan the receptionist came to me another time and said, "It's a quiet day, Carl. I've not seen anybody. There aren't a lot of people in the office today. So, just curious, do you have any other ideas about what I can do to improve my current state? Not sure why, but I'm feeling a little down."

I smiled and said, "Well, remember that quote from Deepak Chopra, that our imagination can serve one of two things—anxiety or creativity. But that's a little too theoretical and I like to distill it down to a practice. Did you know that we apparently can't be anxious or depressed and grateful at the same time? So say any number of psychiatrists, psychologists, and neuroscientists."

"No, I haven't heard that before," she said.

I said, "But again, we don't have to accept someone else's word for it—let's experiment. Here's a fun practice. Take out a piece of paper and note the top twenty things that you're most grateful for, right now, in this moment. They all have to be different. I'll start you off on the top three that I find I'm most grateful about in you." And I said, "The quality of your smile, how attentive and present you are, and your laugh—I just love your laugh! Now, if you feel so inspired, you can take these same three things, start your list, and probe your wonderful mind for seventeen more."

She called me back a little while later and said, "Oh my gosh. At first, I struggled with what to write, but then I took a deep breath, smiled, and relaxed. I remembered you saying the list was for me to play with and not for anyone else to ever see, and then my thoughts poured out of me with ease."

I said, "As a student of your own experience, it can be wonderfully creative to tap into your wisdom and pay conscious attention to the many insights gleaned."

"This was so helpful because when I was doing it, I lost sight of what was bothering me. I just wasn't thinking about it."

"It's called spiraling up," I said. "We're accustomed to spiraling down and misery loving company and so on, but gratitude is an opportunity to sustain a different resonance within yourself and then spiraling up because you're focusing on the different positive aspects of your being. With enough practice you cultivate an attitude of gratitude. The number twenty is a big number. Once you get past five, there's often a moment of uncertainty that you'll make it to twenty. But your own experience helps you see how each point feeds the next. It's also a nice catalyst, because you wouldn't have otherwise believed you could come up with that many. When you do, you feel satisfaction."

When the day was done, I gave Susan another fun challenge: "Have you ever heard of a gratitude journal?" She said no, so I briefly explained this present-moment awareness practice. I said, "When you go to bed, just before your head hits the pillow, write down the top three or top five things you're most grateful for from the day. You can write them or think them, whatever works best for you. It's idiosyncratic. But here's the kicker—every night, they must be unique to the day. Not that there's anything wrong with repeating the same list— but if you really want to deepen the quality of the experience, then go with new examples. See if you can make them novel— something you've never thought to appreciate before—and you'll be shocked at the never-ending list of things that arise. The reason so many choose to write them down is because it's hard to write one thing while thinking of another, so the exercise itself helps you practice present-moment awareness."

Susan said, "You're on."

And I said, "Well, you're on, actually—this will all be thanks to you!"

"Do you do this?"

"I do. When I go to bed, I think of the three things I was most grateful for from the day. And when I wake up, I think of the three things I'm most excited and intentional about." That focuses the reticular activating system (RAS)—a system in our brain that seeks all the relevant data that will help us accomplish what we're intentional about. Our RAS acts like search engine: Whatever intention we input, our brain searches for what will support us accordingly.

Susan started keeping a gratitude journal and about one month later met with me again, excited. "Something wonderful continues to happen, Carl. Not only does the practice make me appreciate my days more, but because I know I'm going to seek new examples every day, I've started programming myself to look for the good, for the things I appreciate. This has dramatically increased how present, observant, and appreciative I am throughout my day. It's honestly magic, how much it has affected my attitude and my presence: the two key components that allow the leader in me to be experienced more often than not. Would it be fair for me to conclude that I'm becoming more mindful? And do you have any other tips for cultivating mindfulness?"

I smiled and shared that her own experience has already answered her first question. And as for any other tips, we discussed how easy it is to lose sight of present-moment awareness, as our minds wander. Mindfulness is being aware of what's filling our mind in any given moment. We can always use our senses to ground ourselves in that moment—a fun way to develop the quality of space between stimulus and response. For instance, the next time you take a walk, practice being conscious of each step. You may notice things you never have before: sensations in your feet, with your balance, in your hips and other joints. And when you do, your focus will be on those sensations and observations and not on any other forms of mental distraction. Any pain associated with some story you may have been ruminating about gives way to your focused attention on what you sense: see, hear, smell, taste, touch. Focusing on your breath can be helpful for the same reason. Since you have to breathe to live, bringing focused attention to your breath grounds you in this moment.

This is relevant because between stimulus and response there's a space. The quality of your leadership is a function of how effectively you use that space. When you are mindful, you are aware of that space where you can be self-reflective. Rather than just shouting out a word or choosing a tone that is reactive and not constructive, you can choose to be supportive and not threatening. Mindfulness combined with compassion, combined with hopefulness and playfulness—these are the four modes of operation that trigger your parasympathetic nervous system, allowing you to stay calm, cool, and collected.

This conversation reminds of an insight my parents once shared with me: "Carl, there's perhaps no such thing as a certainty in life, but if there were, it would be this—you'll always find what you're looking for. Practice looking for the good in people and circumstances and you will find it. Look for the bad and you can find plenty of that too!"

Recall how our intention informs our actions, which in turn determine the quality of our impact. Choose your actions and you choose your consequences.

Acceptance Is the Gateway to Gratitude

I recently had a conversation over lunch with a colleague and friend of mine. He shared with me a highly personal and distressful situation. He was extremely upset, and so I said to him, "I hear you and appreciate how challenging this must be." Then I added, "Recognize, though, that this has no bearing on who you are."

He said, "What are you talking about? Of course it does. I just told you; I'm falling apart."

I said, "I understand, but what I mean is that, in this moment, you're still the wonderful person I've always known you to be." Seeing that he was still perplexed, I continued. "When we first sat down together, the waiter came over and we ordered our drinks—you could clearly see that he didn't know your story, or mine for that matter. There was only his present-moment experience of us. Free of any story of your past, you calmly, politely, and coherently ordered what you wanted with a smile on your face. Your demeanor only changed after he left and you got back to equating who you are with your story. I just wanted to bring that to your attention."

He said, "I still don't get it, Carl. I mean, I'm really distressed."

I said, "Do you trust me?"

He said, "Yes, of course, I do. That's why I'm sharing everything so openly."

I continued, "OK, so listen. I'm about to ask you something that's going to seem incredibly odd, but just trust me, and then we'll circle back around."

He said, "Fine."

I asked him, "I know you're a master carpenter—"

Focus on the experience of you, not the story about you. This helps you accept what is happening in your life and teaches you to not take things for granted but rather as granted.

"Carl," he interrupted, "I'm so sorry, but my heart is breaking. I'm telling you about this horrendous situation, and you're talking to me about my carpentry expertise."

"Just bear with me for a second. This table that we're sitting at—I couldn't help but notice the wood. But what I was curious about is if you rub the surface of it, how would you explain the finish and texture to me? And how do you think they did it?"

He said, "Are you joking?"

I said, "No."

Still bewildered he said, "Fine." And he rubbed the table surface, feeling it and thinking about it. He then explained what kind of wood it was and how it had been sanded and treated. I smiled. And then, after I had acknowledged his expertise and thanked him, just as quickly as that moment had come, he returned to his distraught state.

So, I said, "In those several moments when you were in the present, as you touched the wood and felt the finish, what happened to the suffering that had, only moments earlier, consumed our conversation? Have you ever heard people exclaim how helpful it is to bring your greatest problems into the light of the present moment? What they mean, in literal terms, has to do with the exercise we just conducted—when you were touching the table, you were wholly present with me. And the story was gone temporarily. It was nowhere in your consciousness, so much so that you even joked with me and we laughed together. The energy shift was profound— you were here. Then I noticed how that state of presence disappeared when your story returned to the forefront of your consciousness."

"What does that mean?" he asked.

"It means we're not what we have, nor what we do. We're not our stories. Our energetic expression of pure potentiality, that is who we are; it exists and flows, regardless of these other things. The very essence of who you are is always intact. There isn't a story out there that you could share about yourself that would change the essence of who I know you to be."

I reminded him that if we practice focusing on the experience of us, and not the story about us, then we're liberated from the story. This helps us accept what is happening in our lives, while also teaching us to not take things for granted but rather as granted.

"I always say that acceptance is the gateway to gratitude. As soon as we practice acceptance, gratitude arises. Gratitude for the teachings, for the people in our lives, perhaps for our health. All these simultaneous points of gratitude come across our purview. If you just for a moment accept everything the way it is, is there anything that you could possibly feel gratitude for right now?"

He responded, "Well, I mean, I'm grateful for you. I'm grateful for our friendship."

I said, "Amazing, thank you, and what else?"

"I'm grateful that I can see you and I can hear you and that I was healthy enough to make my way to this table and enjoy this meal together in a safe space."

Without even knowing it, he started to be grateful for his senses—his ability to be—his very existence, if you will. And I said to him, "You know, that's another example of *being* trumping *doing*. Being is primary; doing is a distant second. But if you infuse your being into your doing, look what happens. And you can't do that if you're not conscious and accepting of this moment."

As our conversation continued, he remained present as we appreciated each other and explored endless possibilities for the journey ahead. Possibilities that only a short while earlier would have seemed impossible.

You may have noticed a pattern: compassion, then creativity, and finally courage to plan. The future became interesting again when the weight of the problem gave way to possibility. Needless to say, we both left that afternoon feeling grateful and response-able as a consequence.

Marcel Proust suggested to stop and smell the roses. That's a way to sense our aliveness. Martin Seligman talks about positive psychology and, if we are to flourish, the necessity of PERMA: positive emotion, engagement, relationships, meaning, accomplishments. He also says that of the virtues for flourishing, the top one is zest. Reverence for being. Isn't it amazing that we just get to be!

I like to joke that even Shakespeare was onto this: "To be or not to be, that is the question." Notice he didn't say to be *this* or to be *that*. That came later, from society. Just to be or not to be. So, are you here? Are you present? The more you practice that, the more aware and alive you will be.

Giving Yourself Permission

Will you give yourself permission? People usually respond to that question by saying, "Permission for what?" To be who you are, to hone your focus in pursuit of a meaningful objective, to face a meaningful challenge, to service a need of interest, to simply offer your best and do what you can. The list goes on... So, will you give yourself permission? So many of us do not, but why not? Maybe it's a habit of doing what someone else thought we should do, so we cover up this understanding that we have the power within us—literally, in this moment—to give ourselves permission to write the book, to question the authority in the room, to do whatever we can in service of the moment.

A lack of this type of permission results in many meetings concluding without the wealth of multiple opinions being expressed. How many times have you sat through a meeting and found that no one had any questions or comments? What are the odds that absolutely no one had anything else to offer? When we don't give ourselves permission to be ourselves, we lose our originality, our unique voice, and so our learning and our ability to benefit others is stunted. Is it thanks to fear? Very likely. But once you've spent time with others who not only respect themselves but evidence their respect for you, sharing becomes easier. Disagreement can be met with curiosity and a hope that new learning is about to emerge.

So, I ask, "Can you disagree and not be disagreeable?" It's an interesting question to ponder. If others find you disagreeable, my sense is that you will know this. So the real question is, will you choose to do something constructive about it? Can you disagree and not be disagreeable?

How to Be Intentional

One day, I was visiting a senior executive who's also a friend of mine. I was waiting in his office when he entered flustered, closed the door, leaned his back against the wall, and said, "I'm sorry, but I give up." He was stressed, intense, a little flushed.

I said, "What is it, Pete?"

He said, "Carl, I don't know. Midway through my sentence, Sylvie's chin started to quiver. So, I stopped. I realized I said something wrong, and I tried to backtrack. She looked like a deer caught in headlights. I just didn't know what to do. I adjourned the meeting and let her leave. And now I have no idea what to do."

I said, "You know what? Firstly, congratulations for recognizing somebody's cues. Because the Pete of old would have plowed on anyway, Sylvie would have become a puddle right before your eyes, and you would have rationalized why it was her problem and not yours. This time, you paused, you adjourned the meeting, and now you're choosing to reflect and discuss. That's awesome. So, let's role-play a little and we'll come up with some things you can do." This ended up working well.

Sylvie's quivering chin wasn't a premeditated strategy. As you probably guessed, it was a physical, biological reaction, totally beyond her control (once triggered). She didn't mean to become a deer in the headlights; in fact, I'm sure she actively resisted it. But, say it with me, we feel before we think. Pete too—he didn't mean to ignore Sylvie's feelings and steamroller her. He was just going about his responsibilities the best way he knew, damn the torpedoes. Until one hit his colleague and reduced her to tears.

If, like Sylvie, you're on the receiving end of a less-than-desirable behavior, you might confuse poor impact with ill intent on the part of the other. Most of the time ill intent isn't the issue. Rather, your colleague was simply not intentional to start with and so their actions were less conscious and more reactive—hence the less-than-desirable impact. Knowing this allows you to pause before judging another, consider their intention, and respond from there. Furthermore, you cannot control others, but you can remember the importance of being consciously intentional yourself. Consider the type of impact you would like to have in any given moment, and then ground yourself with intention and actions that align. Why would we ever hand over control of ourselves to another? Keep that privilege to yourself.

Recall the four different mindsets (leader, spectator, cynic, or victim). The biochemistry of our minds and bodies is dramatically different depending upon which lens we are looking through. As for the bridge from intention to impact, our actions will also differ dramatically based on the quality of our emotional state. Any negative emotion that results from a trigger (such as condescension, a lack of support, an unreasonable request, something unfair, and being ignored) can pull you off-center and affect your thoughts and actions, thus breaking down the alignment between your conscious, good intentions and your ultimate impact on yourself and others.

Pete ended up doing a lot of work on being intentional. He became a people's champion, vocally supporting those in the trenches, not making assumptions, and going out of his way to take teams out for dinners and social events to thank them. Previously, he had letter after letter on his personnel file because of how belligerent and difficult he was. That person was no more. But Pete didn't just *think* his way to resolution. He intentionally *acted* to change.

You Experience the World from Within

I have a fun exercise for you to consider and reflect upon. Imagine that you're sitting in a room with me, among any number of friends and colleagues. I look at you and ask, "Do you see me?" Everyone smiles and says of course... to which I respond, "Please point to where you see me." Everyone points a finger straight at me, to which I respond, "Thank you, but that's incorrect." Let's try another question: "Do you hear me?" You and your friends smile and say yes... and I follow this up with "Great, please point to where you hear me." Some in the room (perhaps including you) point to their ears. And then I say, "Correct—and congratulations! Now back to my first question. Do you see me? Where do you see me?" The entire room points to their eyes.

The lesson: We only ever experience the world from within. We never have, never can, and never will experience anything outside of ourselves, outside of our own senses. So, now we can appreciate, perhaps at an even deeper level, why our behavior tells us more about ourselves than the subject we may be speaking about or the person we are speaking to.

The lens you look *out* through is the same one that processes and interprets the incoming data. This hopefully helps you see that you truly do create your own experience. Anything at all could come your way and you can choose to consciously process it in a way that transmutes whatever it is into a more peaceful, loving—and yes, compassionate, creative, and courageous—alternative. If you are attempting to survive a given moment, then survival instincts will be necessary. But with most of your life situations, I hope you'll experiment with this level of awareness and the results you can cocreate when accessing your heart, head, and gut brains, respectively.

One more fun fact: The leader in us practices engaging compassion, mindfulness, hopefulness, and playfulness. Research from Richard Boyatzis suggests that these four qualities activate our parasympathetic nervous system (PNS). When the PNS is activated, renewal results. Our body rebuilds itself neurologically, growing new neural tissue (neurogenesis), engaging our immune system, and becoming healthier and more open to new ideas, emotions, people, and possibilities, learning adaptation and change. Without regular renewal experiences, chronic stress will make our performance unsustainable.

As the leader in us practices operationalizing hope, playfulness, compassion, and mindfulness, we give ourselves the best opportunity for holistic health and well-being. Perhaps not surprisingly, the victim and cynic paradigms have the opposite effect and often trigger the sympathetic nervous system, which prepares our body for momentary all-hands-on-deck survival, depleting our immune system. Unless we really need to be in survival mode, staying in it is harmful to our physiology. We can keep this in mind when visualizing the kind of future we want. So, please consider in your mind's eye options for a hopeful, playful, mindful, and compassionate future.

9

The Expression
of Your Energy

F YOU become dialed in with the quality of your energy and are consistently intentional about your attention— are you covered? That is, will you positively impact more times than not? The litmus test will be in your words, tone of voice, and body language, all three of which must be congruent with your intentions. It's all very well and good to genuinely want to benefit others with your energetic best, but if you don't deliver that intention with sincerity, you expose yourself.

I once conducted a session with an executive group that included someone with a fairly argumentative personality profile. I could tell his relationship with those in attendance was strained. I could see others rolling their eyes and recognized they had little patience for him. He was clearly unaware when it came to his tone, body language, and choice of words, none of which were open, friendly, curious, or constructive. At one point he said, "Well, this has all been really nice: values and values-driven leadership and all these great things. But what I want to know is, what about greed? Greed is a value."

When you dig in and defend against an already defensive posture, you risk both the other person and you being hijacked and digging in further, so that the original point of the discussion becomes secondary or is lost entirely. So, I said, "Sure. Greed is *a* value. The values we have discussed do not constitute an exhaustive list. Rather, our focus has been specific to your company's values, of which there are only six. And my understanding is that—correct me if I'm wrong—they've been chosen consciously based on the kind of culture you want to cultivate and that you aspire to. So, if what you're asking is how does greed fit within your corporate culture, I would just ask all of you how does the expression of greed reconcile with one or several of your other six values?"

Everyone laughed and said, "It doesn't. In fact, it has no place in our organization."

I said, "OK, well then, there's your answer."

Then this individual said, "So, you're saying greed doesn't exist?"

I said, "No, I'm simply pointing out that greed isn't a viable option within your aspirational corporate culture—your company's brand will not support it. However, let's imagine that greed is your number one personal value. Well, I'd suggest then that you have one of two choices. You can either rationalize how greed fits within the six values we've discussed, which you and your peers have just said is impossible, or you can choose to leave this organization and hang your own shingle—you could even promote greed as your number one value. And then you'll attract others who would share in kind. That's partly how you cultivate a certain culture."

He said, "Carl, that is the only answer I would have accepted. I thought that all along but wanted to see how you would handle my inquiry, so congratulations."

Fascinating to me that he struggled to collaboratively say something like, "Got it. OK, thanks." He had to frame it as if it were a test and that he knew the answer all along. Not a recommended approach for creating resonance—or trust.

Afterward, many people apologized to me, for him, in private. He came up to me too and said, "I just want to tell you how incredible this was."

"Thank you," I said.

"I've heard people talk about this before, but you really get it and you know how to shape it in a way that made it practical, and I just wanted to celebrate that fact now."

Some of you may be thinking, "There's no way he was going to say that in front of anyone else," and you might be right. It's possible that he only did it because he knew his boss is the one who hired me to help the team. I still responded with thanks and told him how much I appreciated his positive feedback (which I did). In the back of my mind, I also reminded myself that no one is difficult from a position of strength. So, hopefully, our workshop allowed him to be in a better place, where the leader in him stepped up while the victim or cynic took a rest.

Two senior executives approached me after everyone else had left and shared that the exchange I had had with their colleague fascinated them. They wanted to understand how it was that I did not seem to let my ego get in the way, particularly when he was so aggressive. I shared that the work is about role modeling what I hope to receive from others, being intentional about my attention. "I'm just here to share from what I've experienced and learned, from what I've been taught and have taught, and give the best I've got in service of that objective. And if you find that helpful in some shape or form, great. If you don't, that's OK too. You just won't invite me back. I will still know I gave you my best."

If you reflect on this exchange for a moment, you can see how quickly bonds can either be formed or compromised. The body language of the room clearly indicated that this particular team member had very little support. To me, that's sad. Yes, his behavior and how he expressed himself are likely mirrored back to him more often than not, perpetuating his bitterness and encouraging him to double down on being difficult. But think of the cost to the business, to the relationships, to the underlying trust—and to the wasted energy all this produces, not to mention the toxic contagion that results. Now imagine his behavior has become a trait—and you report to him. How long will you choose to last? And how much will you want to give?

Feeling like the Only Person in the Room

A senior manager approached me and said, "I'm about to meet with the CEO. I'm terrified, Carl. This person is the leader of a multibillion-dollar multinational organization, and I have no idea how to handle how I'm feeling. Do you have any advice?"

I grinned and repeated a saying my father often used, "Well, I don't give advice, Janet, because what do I know? I'm just a rookie. But I do have a few suggestions, if you're interested? A few things that might be helpful to think about."

She smiled and said, "Absolutely, please!"

I said, "Well, as CEO, she is the top leader in the land of this company's culture. If she is as wonderful as I imagine she must be to have ascended to that level of formal authority, then surely this is going to be the easiest meeting you have ever had. So, let's park the fear, because the meeting will consist of her being fully engaged with you, 100 percent present;

she'll be very practiced at making sure that you're the most important person in the room, because you're the only person in the room. How does that make you feel?"

Janet said, "I'm excited just thinking about it. But let's be honest. What if that doesn't happen?"

"If it doesn't happen, then clearly you're not the one with the lesson to learn."

That allowed Janet to give herself permission to expect (and appreciate) good things. And if they weren't as good as hoped, then instead of being a victim of that circumstance, she could be an observer, and she could become a student of the experience, thinking, "Wow, she is the CEO of this remarkable company and seems to have little concept of how she's showing up right now. Maybe I can help her or make things a little easier, or maybe I can promote a little bit of candor or show a little courage." That attitude keeps you in the driver's seat of your own energy. It allows the leader in you to still be present and accounted for, instead of defaulting to spectator, cynic, or victim.

Janet used that lesson not only in that meeting but in other meetings with people senior to her. Every time she encountered difficulty, she would think to herself, "Wow, does this person ever have an opportunity to learn more about themselves." And every one of those "lessons to learn" distilled to one key proposition: How do you consciously practice being aware of the experience you cocreate with every person you encounter?

What is it like to be in your presence?

If the answer is "it's really fun, uplifting, interesting, insightful," the odds are good others will want to see you again.

Emotional contagion is real. I remember hearing that our bodies can pick up on another's energy in less than a second, and that we have about thirty seconds before another's dominant emotional state becomes our own—unless we are aware enough to self-regulate accordingly. Even if my quality of energy is high and my focus is intentional, if I do not express myself effectively, my impact upon others may be less than desirable. The quality of the experience we have with one another will also determine our level of engagement and will influence our desire to see each other again.

So, ask yourself this key question again: What's it like to be in your presence? Are you a calming, reflective force, an inspirational voice who encourages the weary, or does your skepticism and cynicism beat people down? Do you lift others up with your optimism or drag them down with your world-weary negativity? Do other team members feel heard, seen, valued, and appreciated when they are with you? In a nutshell, are they having fun? Does your name on the call display evoke excitement or fear?

Being mindful of the energy you bring to every interaction—its quality, focus, and expression—will make all the difference.

Verbal Language, Body Language, and Focus

Verbal language (inclusive of words and tone), body language, and the focus of our attention are three primary drivers that affect our emotional states. Awareness of all three will allow us to course-correct when under pressure and have ready-made alternatives available to ensure we don't compromise our level best.

Our words matter. Words are things. The effects of receiving less than kind words can reverberate for years. I have heard that of the just over 76,000 most common words in the English dictionary, four thousand connote emotion.

Guess what proportion of the four thousand are positive? If you guessed 10 percent, you are correct. With 90 percent of those words being less than desirable, choosing our words wisely is so important. That so many words are negative is an interesting commentary on where we, as a society, tend to focus our talk.

Everything I reference here about how we might approach one another is equally important for ourselves. In your self-talk, are you positive, kind, compassionate, understanding, forgiving, encouraging? Many are not. No better time to practice. The language we choose shapes the pathways in our brain, so please choose your words consciously, for everyone's sake. We form habits of speech and language, so it's only rational to select words that work for us and those in our presence.

Not surprisingly, the second contributor to our emotional state is our physiology, otherwise known as body language. Most of us have heard about how important it is to listen to more than words when attempting to understand one another. What does a colleague's body language tell you? Recall the last time you felt on top of the world—what was your body doing? Standing tall, smiling, breathing deeply, with eyes bright. Contrast this with moments when you have felt less than optimal—how did your body interpret this state? Head down, shoulders slumped, eyes glazed... You get the picture.

Did you know that being mindful of your current posture and positioning yourself to reflect how you would carry yourself if you felt at your best can transform your current mental state? Try shifting your body language to mirror your most admirable traits. Does anything happen?

Lastly, your *focus* will affect your emotional state. Where do you concentrate your attention? Are you intentional about

Do you consciously practice being aware of the experience you cocreate with others?

your attention? Practicing living in the present allows you to live with presence. And ruminating about the past or being lost in the future risks losing this present moment—the only moment through which your energy is available to flow.

My father helped me understand this more tangibly when he once asked, "Carl, who would you say is the most important person in your life?" To which I responded, "Well, Dad, you would be pretty high up there," and then continued listing my mom and siblings. His response was a fun one: "What if I suggested that you practice making it the person who happens to be in front of you at any given moment? Because you see, Son, in that moment, they're the only person in your life, so you may as well practice making them the most important one. And in their mind, they are." Practice this and explore what impact it has on the quality of your relationships.

Recall that your natural state—in which you operate at peek proficiency, physiologically speaking—is compassionate, mindful, hopeful, and playful (reflecting your unique sense of humor). If you're not in your natural state, then you are resisting something. What? you may ask. It doesn't matter because we know where resistance leads. What we resist persists. Practice compassion, offer service, but do not offer to make their issue your issue. This would take you away from the present moment and weaken your presence, your resolve, and your effectiveness. Shoulder in support, but focus on thoughts and actions associated with your natural state. To lose your awareness of this moment is to miss out on life itself... and life is too short for that.

Practicing greater awareness across all three of these areas can dramatically impact your life and the influence you have with others. Just imagine if you were to filter your words and actions before responding, allowing your body language to reflect your positivity and purpose, while also giving your full attention to the moment. It's not hard to see the impact this would have on your reality.

Again, time for practice. In your next conversation, be mindful of the words you choose. How did your conscious choices shape the mutual experience of the moment? Then do it again, but this time focus on your body language and look for any change in experience. Lastly, practice giving your full attention to your next conversation. Listen intently and pause and reflect before responding. What did you notice? Repeat and build on what worked best while experimenting to see if other aspects could use some fine-tuning. Have fun with the process and celebrate how each attempt is evidence of progress.

The Experience (Not the Story) of You

You can either choose to focus on *the story about you*, or you can choose to focus on *the experience of you*. If you choose the story, which happens to be what the world is conditioning you to choose via social media and so on, then just know that you will come to believe that you are what you do and you are what you have—when, of course, you are neither. But say that to the average person and they'll disagree, until they give it more thought. As I say to my kids, you know who you are is who you are.

Here's how I've seen it play out. When you focus on the story of your life, just remember that every time a variable of the story (or a character in it) changes, you're going to think you've been forced to change. And most people are not very good at managing change in an open, holistic, compassionate, empathetic way. So, here's the deal—focusing on the experience of who you are is going to liberate you, from the chains of the story, from what others say, and more. But if you choose to focus on the story instead, OK. It's your choice. But at least remember—you're the author! You're the narrator! So, please write a story that works for you and for those that you share this life with.

The anxiety for people to somehow have all the answers is getting worse these days. One of the happiest occasions in the lives of university students, according to some research, is the day they learn they've been admitted to an institution of their choice. It could be the school they picked or one somebody in their family aspired to, Ivy League or otherwise—it doesn't matter. The day they find out? Wow, they're living the dream.

Do you know what stage in the university lifecycle has the highest incidence rate of depression among students? The start of second year. In first year, all is still euphoric. And then sets in the reality of how hard it is, of questioning if they really want it, of the dropout rates, and of "what if I don't make it through the weed-out?"

Graduates, at least, can say, "Well, I've got a ticket. Now it's up to me—I don't know what I'm going to do, but I've got something." But those second-year students often start to substitute the essence of who they are with their story, which in their heads could be a scary story of failure or wrong paths—and that story becomes so important that a lot of them lose their sense of self.

What if they were only told to live into the answers instead? In his famous Stanford commencement speech, Steve Jobs said, "Trust that the dots will connect at some point." Which is just another way of saying, honor the experience of life. Make *being* primary and *doing* a distant second, because you know that if you invest the best of who you are in whatever you do, that's the best you've got to give.

The Essence of You

I've often asked executive teams, "Give me an example of something that could happen outside you that could affect your originality, the essence of who you are."

After some thought, they often reply, "Nothing."

And I say, "Exactly. Nothing. Because you're an original. There will never be another one of you. The question is, are you going to be respectful of that and the voice that it affords you, the perspective, the point of view?" Many people lose sight of that, pretending to be someone or something they're not. But that energy expression is already spoken for, and they don't realize that everybody loses when you express yourself inauthentically.

One person said to me, "You've been so successful. How can I be successful?"

And I said, "You know, the simplest suggestion is not to focus on being successful but to focus on being valuable. It's such a simple nuance. To literally focus on adding incremental value with every interaction. And by the way, I have a question for you."

"Sure, what's that, Carl?"

"How will you know that you're adding incremental value to the person you're hoping to serve?"

They paused for a second and said, "Well, I guess I could ask them what they need."

I said, "Exactly. Confirm the need and then ask them what would value look like, feel like, sound like. And then service it."

All Common Sense?

Some people say to me that this is all common sense. I often respond, "Maybe, but in my experience, common sense that is not commonly practiced." There is great news though. If you commonly practice modeling the attributes that matter and avoiding the ones that don't, then you will have a track record a mile long. You will be the most sought-after coach, mentor, confidante, leader, boss. So, you need to be honest with yourself. Pause for a moment... look around... listen... If you're not in demand, then there's likely more to do. You may not be practicing those EI attributes so often after all.

Every time you hear yourself saying, "This is common sense," question whether you are role modeling in kind. Ask, "Am I modeling my best, day to day?" That sounds so commonsensical, and I think you'll probably find that in many instances—not all, but in many—you're not. The upside is that, thanks to your honesty, you'll discover an opportunity to make common your common sense.

The wonderful part is when you stay open, experiment, and see what might produce a better answer for you and those around you, know this: Inherent within each new attempt is hope. Hope that the next option may allow for more of your best to be shared and received by those you have the privilege to lead.

In conclusion, most of the attributes that define exceptional leaders, and poor leaders alike, fall within EI. I'm reminded of a quote attributed to Maya Angelou: "I've learned that people will forget what you said, people will forget what you did, but people will never forget how you made them feel."

Are great leaders perfect in this regard? No. Leadership is not about perfection. But great leaders do practice being aware of how people feel when they're around them, knowing that's what others will remember most. When it comes to your own leadership, how do you do in this regard? How is this affecting your impact? The sooner you answer these questions, the sooner you can promote a higher level of self-awareness that will improve your ability to self-manage. By improving the quality, focus, and expression of your energy, you improve the capacity, effort, and impact of your abilities.

10

Practice Makes Progress

C LOSE TO twenty years ago, I teamed with a new administrative assistant, Judith. She was very quiet, kind, and timid. She used to explain that her family was originally from a country that was responsible for her subservient approach toward formal authority. When we first met, she was a bit overwhelmed. She told me later that although I was nothing but kind to her, at first she couldn't quite believe it— she had heard that I was a friendly and trusting person but had often experienced people who had ulterior motives, so she was suspicious. Fair enough.

When she retired, after almost thirty years, she spoke of our teaming together in a beautiful card she gave to me. In it she said, "My dearest Carl ... You have been such an inspiration. I have learned so much from your trust as well as your leadership skills. You turned/influenced/taught me to grow from the shy and quiet employee to becoming the more outgoing and confident person people meet today. In fact, many of my coworkers were commenting that, at my retirement party, I gave the nicest speech they'd ever heard. At the time

I kept telling myself, as long as I behave like Carl does, surely I'll be all right. Because you don't just speak, you speak from your heart. I can't tell you how much this has transformed me. I am going to miss you more than my heart can express."

Why would I share such a personal note? Because Judith's transformation fed my own. Here she was thanking me, but the growth, admiration, and learning went both ways. We focused on true teamwork, on the dynamic goals of cocreating experiences that were enjoyable, that helped others, and that facilitated learning from all that came our way. While others may have referred to their assistants as assistants, I referred to Judith as my business partner.

All I ever did for Judith was mirror back to her how great she was. Every time she apologized, sold herself short, and said, "I could have done this" or "I should have done that," I'd say, "Judith, did we make progress? Yes, we made progress. I just want to celebrate that we progressed. You keep wanting perfection, and I just want progress. Every day we show up, we progress. And that's what I'm going to celebrate." What a joy, what a privilege—we can express how we matter to one another. Do those who support you know how much they matter to you?

EVERYTHING IS practice—to make progress, not perfection. Lawyers and doctors "practice medicine" or "practice law," like they're playing and learning on the job. Before you go out and play a hockey game, you practice. In a way, that's what work is too. We're practicing, and hopefully learning from our mistakes while progressing.

During a golf game, a gentleman in my foursome was upset with his game. As we were going to the tenth tee he said, "You know what? The front nine was just practice; now it's time to play golf."

I smiled and said, "Since neither one of us does this for a living, and even if we did, I'm pretty sure it's all practice." He just laughed. "That's so funny. That is such a great way to look at playing the game. I used to think that only the driving range was practice, but you're saying it's all practice." I said, "Always. Everything."

That's why I love the expression "practice makes progress." If you're talking about neuroscience, practice can also make permanent, in terms of the new neural pathways that you want to grow and that become your new habits. Now, it's never permanent indefinitely because of neuroplasticity. But remember, neurons that fire together wire together. The more you practice something, the more the myelin sheath develops. Neurosurgeon Sanjay Gupta writes, "The brain can be constructively changed—enhanced and fine-tuned. You can affect your brain's thinking and memory far more than you realize or appreciate, and the vast majority of people haven't even begun to try."

What are you practicing? Are you practicing misery, or are you practicing possibility? A lot of people don't even realize how often they focus on what they don't want as opposed to what they do want. Practice complaining enough and you can become an expert at it.

The only perfect thing about you is that you are a manifestation of life itself. An original, one-of-a-kind, unique amalgam of life experience—in that regard, there's nothing that can touch your originality. But in terms of evolving as beings, as creatures that learn and expand energetically and intellectually and lovingly, it just never ends. There's no limit to it. No ultimate boundary. Energy itself can never disappear or be destroyed; it just changes form.

The etymology of the word "confident" is "intense trust." In what? In your ability to contribute meaningfully to the moment. So, the more you can help people become witness to their ability to contribute meaningfully, and then to do as they say, guess what happens? Their confidence grows.

Show Up and Contribute

My former company has a lot of co-op students, and I was often the partner to talk with them in open forums. I would say, "I'm going to share some insight that I hope you will reflect upon."

"What's that?" they would ask.

"Well, this is going to sound really funny, but you do all know that you're adults, right?" We would share a good laugh amid the apparent confusion of the question. And then while exchanging glances with one another, someone would always ask, "What?"

Then I would say, "Why did you join this organization?" We would talk about the why, and about what part of the mission resonated with them. Then we would discuss their strengths and interests, and how would they like to put them into service. And then I would add, "While you're putting your skills into service, you do realize that you're an adult? One with a point of view about how we do things. Be curious about that. Nuance your point of view. Remember, as our newest team members, you have the freshest lens of anyone about the way we do things."

"OK. Sure. But why do you remind us that we're all adults?"

"Because as soon as you land here, some really weird things happen," I would reply. "You somehow think that just because someone is 'senior' to you, that they take on more of a parental role, where you simply have to accept what they

In terms of evolving as beings,
as creatures that learn and expand
energetically and intellectually
and lovingly, it just never ends.
There's no limit to it.

say, just because they said it. It's one thing to role model respect, but it's another to undervalue yourself, think to yourself that you have nothing to offer, and stay silent when the very thing we might need most is your wisdom, the power of your questioning. I never want you to forget that. If you have a question or a curiosity, express it. Be professional, be respectful, and express it."

They would often reply with "Wow! Really?" I had given them permission. That's the word. I often find myself saying, "Will you give yourself *permission* to show up and contribute, in whatever form that takes, the best version of what you have to offer? Come what may? Will you give yourself permission to do that?" That's what it all boils down to.

The flip side is to ask the same question of a company's leaders: "Are you, as leaders, all the way down the hierarchical pyramid, giving your team members permission to ask those questions, especially the hard ones?"

"You bet," they reply. OK, great. So, how do you foster that, plant it, make it grow, nurture it? Well, you ask the open-ended, hard questions. And because some people might be like the Judiths of the world, a little quieter, you might need to cultivate it. With Judith, I would say, "Hey, Judith, believe me, you are far more the expert in this space than I am." And I'd pick an area where clearly she was the expert, and I'd say, "I know very little about this. Would you mind if I were to do this at home on the weekend, can you give me a few tips?"

She would reply, "Well, who am I to talk to you as a partner? But, I must admit, I am an expert in this space. So this is what I like to do first, second, and third."

And then what would I do? First thing on Monday morning, I'd say, "Judith, you are golden. Those tips, that sequence, brilliant. Never shy away from giving me tools and tips and tactics like that again, because, wow, what a difference it makes. And Julie, my wife, and my kids, Scott and Haley, thank you too—because thanks to your tips I was able to make it to the show with all of them."

She would laugh, quietly, but over time, her voice developed and turned into "Carl, by the way, don't forget to do this, don't get lost, always save this." She was teaching me, taking the bull by the horns, and I loved it.

Remember Google's Project Aristotle, which concluded that teams need psychological safety? Further recall that we feel before we think. So, how are you feeling? How are your feelings informing your thoughts? How are your feelings and thoughts informing your actions? How are your feelings and thoughts and actions informing the experience someone just had of working with you?

In my experience, I've observed the power of the three *a*'s: affection, appreciation, and attention. As was the case with Judith and me, the more consciously you practice putting these into action (action is perhaps the fourth *a*), the greater your level of connection. Showing you care, expressing gratitude, and learning to listen are invaluable ways of deepening the quality of any relationship.

On this last point I note that hearing is one of our five senses, but listening is a skill. To sincerely listen to another is a gift. Not only does it validate someone and their distinctive point of view (seeing them by virtue of listening attentively), but it also expands our understanding, clarifies context, and shapes a perspective that can be used to help as needed.

I also often invoke the 7-38-55 rule: Effective communication is composed of 7 percent words, 38 percent tone of voice, and 55 percent body language. Notice how this rule overlaps with my earlier points about our words, body language, and quality of focus. Our words are critically important, but if our tone is supportive and our body language encouraging, then others are very generous regarding our choice of words. And if our tone is discouraging and body language intimidating, even the perfect words will not be believed.

I was once a facilitator at a coaching workshop with a large group of senior managers. When the attendees broke into smaller rooms to practice their presentation skills, I was asked to observe a group in a particular room and to provide feedback on their performances. When I opened the door to enter, everyone in the room looked at me in silence and then started to laugh. You see, we recognized each other, and this was the breakout room for all the French-speaking attendees. The laughter arose because they knew I do not speak French (nor understand it, although I do love the language). After waiting for a bilingual coach to show up and learning there were none available, we decided that I would still sit in, have some fun, and observe. An experiment to see if I could rely on their tone of voice and body language to make some hopefully interesting and helpful insights.

Four pages of notes later, when it came time to debrief, they were astounded by the accuracy of my translation. Even as they spoke French, I could pinpoint their states and resulting levels of nervousness, and where they were at ease with the content or less sure of what they were sharing. It was a wonderful experience and lesson for all of us. For my part, I learned how positively impactful it can be to communicate in your preferred language. Most of these individuals, who were all bilingual, had been quiet during the larger group sessions, but they sprung to life in an environment where they could express themselves openly and fluently. It was like seeing two different versions of each personality. I always keep this in mind whenever I meet someone who does not use English as their go-to language. Observe them using their preferred language and watch the true essence of who they are shine.

PULLING TOGETHER everything we've discussed so far, I'll draw on something Daniel Siegel shared in his "Neuroscience of Change" talk: "Feeling a particular way (from within the energy and information flow arising within our body) is an internal state that we express externally via our emotions. So, our emotion is an external expression (motion) that emanates from how we interpret our internal state/feelings."

In other words, how we feel matters, and yes, it is affected by the quality, focus, and expression of our energy. Pay attention to all three and it will be tough to have a bad day; ignore one, two, or all three and expect to pay the price. On the other hand, even when we're dialed in, if we feel threatened, we risk losing access to our best intellect unless we understand how to mitigate the hijack.

Should you happen to feel less than your best at any given moment, pause and quickly check the quality and focus of your energy. If they seem sound, ask yourself how you have recently expressed yourself to others—if the answer is "less than my best," some humility coupled with an apology might be just what the doctor ordered.

PART III

BIOLOGY SUGGESTS THAT YOUR ACTIONS MATTER

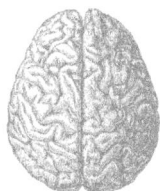

11

What Do Your Actions Say about You?

I N *POSITIVE Psychology and the Body*, psychologist Kate Hefferon notes how she and Nanette Mutrie identified physical activity as a "stellar" positive psychology intervention because of its ability to reduce risk, alleviate ill health, and produce positive emotions, self-efficacy, mastery, and overall flourishing. Exercise has been found to lower the risk of developing "obesity, cardiovascular disease, coronary heart disease, stroke, diabetes (type 2), osteoporosis, certain sleep disorders, high blood pressure (e.g., blood pressure reduces for up to 12 hours post exercise), certain cancers (colon, breast, rectal, lung, prostate, endometrial) and even premature death." It can also enhance immune system functioning, and has been linked to our experiences of well-being, "including positive emotions, self-esteem, body image, cognitive functioning, psychological wellbeing, posttraumatic growth, flow, purpose in life and many, many more concepts."

The physical benefits of action are well known, but its positive effects on our states of mind are less obvious but fascinating too. Be a student of your own experience and test this out. I think you'll find that a focus on learning can feed your esteem and confidence.

You Can Act Your Way into Believing

We mostly believe our way into action. But did you know we can also act our way into believing—that we have bidirectional capacity? This knife cuts both ways.

I remember speaking with an Olympic champion swimmer about his training program. Six days out of seven he had to wake up at 3:30 a.m. to make it to the pool for his 4:15 start. How many of those six days did he "feel" like getting up, battling the elements to get to the pool, and then jumping into chilly water? If you guessed zero, you would be correct.

But once his workout was completed, how many times did he feel good after the work was done? If you guessed six this time, you would be correct. And not only did he feel better than when he started, his attitude was better too: a strong, optimistic, can-do, bring-it-on mantra all his own. But there was more. This improved attitude also affected his belief in himself, his trust that he could deliver consistently all that he had committed to.

So, yes, your beliefs set the context for your attitude, which informs your emotions, behaviors, actions, and results—but just remember that you can reverse that pattern. Some of the most effective coaches teach that when you're feeling your worst, following your protocol and doing your best is most important. Show up, give what you can, and see how this too can impact the world around you in wonderful ways.

IN HIS bestseller *Atomic Habits*, James Clear shares, "Building better habits isn't about littering your day with life hacks... Ultimately, your habits matter because they help you become the type of person you wish to be. They are the channel through which you develop your deepest beliefs about yourself. Quite literally, you become your habits."

And who do you suppose will cultivate the habits that are best for you? The leader in you, the cynic, the spectator, or the victim? When I ask, "What would the leader in you do or say?" you know that your answer will be remarkably different from that of the other three mindsets. And we know that an individual's perception and response to life events can substantially affect their hormonal, neural, and physiological functions: their biology. When you speak and act in a way that reflects the best of you, and practice this enough, watch the best version of yourself arise. Your character references your traits, which as we know are a function of your practiced and repeated states. So actions matter—their consistency, their nature, and their intention.

Dr. Stephen Porges explains that our physiological state is a fundamental part, and not a correlate, of our emotion or mood. According to his polyvagal theory, the state of our autonomic nervous system determines how safe and connected we feel. We will reflexively evaluate the same environmental cues as neutral, positive, or threatening, depending on our physiological state. Biologically, a change in our nervous state will shift access to different structures in the brain, swing us from a social communication mode to the defensive behaviors of fight-or-flight or shutdown. Polyvagal theory emphasizes a bidirectional link between brain and viscera, which explains how thoughts change physiology and physiology influences thoughts. As you change your

Let life play you.
Remain present, give your
best in service of a need,
and life may conspire
for your benefit.

facial expression, voice, breathing pattern, and posture, you also change the neural pathways to the heart.

In Sanjay Gupta's *Keep Sharp*, he shares that "you can change your brain for the better or worse through behaviors and even ways of thinking. Bad habits have neural maps that reinforce those bad habits... Negative thoughts and constant worrying can promote changes in the brain that are associated with depression and anxiety. Repeated mental states, where you focus your attention, what you experience, and how you respond to situations indeed become neural traits."

So, yes, the neuroscientists agree. Feelings, energy, and actions all arise from and affect your biology. Becoming more aware of this allows you to do something constructive about it—to benefit you and all those you spend time with.

Let Life Play You

One of my first employment opportunities was in a warehouse, on an assembly line, for a large multinational company that manufactured goods to be assembled and eventually packed into boxes that were glued shut. I got a position at the end of the line, ensuring the packaging was complete before sealing the boxes with a sophisticated glue machine. And then at the end of the day, I had to clean the glue machine— to make sure everything was set so that we could start fresh the next morning, with no delays.

I was so grateful for the opportunity but nervous in the beginning, hoping I wouldn't let anyone down and not sure I could handle what was to come, because I didn't have any related experience. I had no reason to believe that I would do well in this role—mind you, I had no reason to believe I couldn't do well. In essence, I was hoping I could act (and practice) my way into believing in myself, be it in this role or any other in the warehouse.

In the beginning, some people were tough on me. I was OK with that. After all, I was a university kid, a summer student working among seasoned veterans. I decided that I was going to just give my very best, right down to things like breaks. At first, they would tell me it's break time and I'd say, "Oh, I'm OK." And they'd demand, "Take your break." I was trying to show them my work ethic—but they made it clear, "We get your work ethic, but take the break right now." Initially, I concluded (simplistically) that the insistence must be a union dictate, but I soon learned that the breaks were crucial to sustaining our focus, minimizing mistakes, and avoiding injury. This early lesson served me well over the years that followed. Intentional rest and restoration proved critical to staying healthy amid (at times) a profoundly unhealthy corporate world.

For the first ten days I ate lunch by myself, sitting alone in the lunchroom. If management needed an extra shift done, they'd tell me, "Oxholm, we need a worker tonight," and I'd do it, no problem. I was focused on being present and bringing a helpful energy and on not being distracting or wasteful.

Then, slowly but surely, my coworkers started to observe that I cherished the relationships (and friendships) that we were developing, devoid of judging one another and genuinely practicing gratitude for each opportunity. And some interesting things started to happen. People started inviting me to their tables. They started to share with me in confidence and ask my opinion about things that could positively influence their day and even their work performance.

One person came to me and said, "I never graduated high school, but I've elevated my role in the warehouse to dealing with some of the chemical compounds and everything I do gets reviewed by our manager. I sometimes struggle with the metric conversions and I'm afraid to say something. Do you have any ideas for me?" I appreciate how hard it can be to ask for help, especially when so often we fear someone's judgment of us—so I was thrilled when my coworker trusted me enough to approach me.

And I could help him, first of all to understand how to do the conversions. And then I asked whether he thought the company would benefit from a training program that helped future team members know how to deal with some of the unique aspects of management within the warehouse. Training was already in place, but it was fairly ad hoc. This team member went on to develop a "how to" manual and program for those advancing in their responsibilities—talk about catalyzing fear into productivity for the benefit of all. Observing his initiative taught me never to assume that "someone else" is handling something, along with the value of encouraging others to trust their experience, their voice, and their great ideas. I also learned how to see challenges as about more than an individual and to seek solutions that can help the whole organization. My coworker was later excited to share that he had received a considerable bonus for his idea, which was credited with reducing organizational risk and elevating engagement. Of course, it helped that senior members of the team were willing to celebrate the contributions that came from others, rather than taking the credit for themselves.

Before summer's end I had developed enough trust with my team members that they were comfortable asking me to take on more responsibility, which developed my confidence. Despite limited knowledge in the beginning, I saw I could work my way into more opportunity—albeit in small, incremental steps—but they were significant to me.

My parents had always instilled in me, "When you are bringing your best to what you do, Carl, then it can be interesting to let life play you. If, by remaining present and giving your best in service of a need, life (in the form of others) may have a way of conspiring for your benefit." This started a pattern of thinking and an approach that I enjoy experimenting with to this day. I practice never taking the generosity of others for granted and do my best to ensure my actions are reflective of this.

In other words, I practice staying open, even when a particular thought might occur to me to shut down, judge, close off, or resist. Opportunities will show up, and when they do, I want to habitually infuse my best into what I do. When I've experienced others who are masterful at this open-mindedness, it always inspires me to join their team. My hope is, if I act accordingly, maybe I can affect others in a similar, positive way. If I'm not a fit for what they need, maybe they'll counsel me to another area of opportunity. This option likely only arises if I do my part to evidence an attitude of gratitude and a work ethic to match.

I recall the day when the foreman of the warehouse commented, "Carl, someone could eat dinner off the glue machine every night when you are done with it. Keep up the great work." I felt so responsible for making sure the next person would have clean equipment. I never wanted an assembly line shut down because of something I could have done better. I was quickly learning that our team's success was also my success.

Which led to another massive "aha" moment for me. That same summer, they hired three other summer students to work on the assembly line, in the same role I had. And quickly fired them. What could lead to that level of turnover?

I propose that it had nothing to do with their *ability* to do the job (in fact, I witnessed as much). Rather each respective new hire reported that they were getting bored on the line and with cleaning the glue machine each night. They weren't paying attention and were making mistake after mistake. Why might they have been so uninterested and dismissive of the role? As it turned out, they believed the role was beneath them.

That was a huge wake-up call for me. I never thought that my role was anything other than being respectful, grateful, and focused on the task at hand, so I could bring the best of myself in service of the moment and positively influence the team as a whole—not to mention consciously wanting to add value (the key ingredient for cocreating our success). I was hopeful that I would learn that I was capable of contributing meaningfully and develop more confidence. Among the four of us (me and the three who had been fired), the opportunity before us was the same, but our attitudes were clearly different.

Later, when we had the company golf day, my coworkers from the plant asked if I would golf with them and sit with them at dinner—a genuine gift of friendship that meant so much to me. Even though most are long since retired now, many of us remain dear friends.

This early experience taught me about a process that would help me be of value to others; it started with me first showing how much I valued them and the opportunity. Together we were better; we had more fun; we produced more, learned more, and grew more. We were a true, trusting, got-your-back team. When you find yourself genuinely pulling for others on your team and enjoying their success as you do your own, you won't settle for less; you will find joy in pushing them and in being pushed to reach your respective bests. The various ways we all supported and believed in one another that summer was wonderful, and it needed to be experienced to be believed. Perhaps my coworkers' additional asks, born out of trust, support, and friendship, were evidence of life playing me (conspiring for my benefit). Or perhaps that expression was just a made-up suggestion my parents shared to help me stay open, curious, and committed to my best. Either way, if my focus involves sharing my best while helping you discover yours, it's a joyful way to be.

So tell me, when you reflect on your current experience, what do your actions say about who you are and, ultimately, what you believe?

12

The Kind of Action Life Rewards

COMPANIES MEASURE the productivity of senior leaders by how much money they bring in. So, you may be thinking, "Being magnanimous and helping out other people probably doesn't pay. Why should I do it?"

Here's the funny thing—it *does* pay. It pays multiples. You are rewarded through the early, mid-, and even more senior years of your tenure for what you and those in your charge produce. And then executive leadership and perhaps ownership come along, and you go from being a senior manager who makes $100,000 to an executive/owner who could make a million, a tenfold impact. I'm guessing you'll agree that this only makes sense if you create ten times the value relative to what you created when you were the senior manager!

How confident would you be that your actions produced that multiple? If you don't like your answer, it will not bode well for your sense of confidence, humility, team building, mentoring, and coaching. I've coached many a professional with an initial tendency to focus exclusively on themselves, their own numbers, and their own path while not ensuring that those in their care are thriving. Many keep doing what they did in previous roles (perhaps adding more hours) and thinking, "Now I'm an owner/partner/senior executive, so it's OK that I'm at this pay scale." But some inner inkling betrays them. It's a real knock on one's confidence; it doesn't feel right.

I've spoken to many partners in many different industries who have never reconciled their increase in remuneration. My dad often talked about the Peter Principle: If we're not the wiser, we will be promoted to our level of incompetence. Just because you thrive in one role, it does not always follow that you'll be excellent in another—especially in that big leap from management to formal leadership and/or ownership. And since many appointed "leaders" mistakenly think they're there to give all the answers and tell people what to do, their ability to create an ever-growing multiplier decreases.

But the ones who have reconciled themselves with their new roles as leaders—and backed up their responsibilities with actions—easily talk about future prospects, pay expectations, and the related rationale. They inspire others to stretch and enjoy the powerful, positive difference they can collectively bring to their clients. Because true leaders create a multiplier, through their impact on tens or hundreds of people and by inspiring and guiding thousands. Those are the ones who genuinely are followed—not just because of their formal authority.

If your actions are not helping others make believers out of themselves and showing them that together you can change the world for the better, then you're very possibly spending a lot of energy constantly convincing yourself that you're worth your pay. Many managers land significant opportunities for their organization purely because of the brand itself or their position. In other words, that work was coming to the organization anyway. These folks will be sure to point out (often by expending tremendous amounts of energy) that they alone are the reason for these wonderful opportunities. The ones who build up others one experience at a time, who find joy in being of service, and who measure their success by the success of those they have the privilege to lead—well, they don't need to spend any extra energy to convey their value. Just ask their team members and the clients their teams service—the feedback will say it all.

If you don't develop net-new skills that are leadership oriented, the odds are that you will just have a new title with the same skills you always had, which does not bode well for your long-term impact. Imagine you're now a partner making a multiple of what you earned prior to your promotion last week. What will you do differently? How will you create the multiple that you're now earning? Good questions to have answers to; in most successful cases, the answers will relate to how many others you can inspire to discover and contribute their best for the benefit of others.

I've even said to people, "Let's be very, very clear. This isn't a nice-to-have conversation, this is a must-have actualization: You must be ten times the value that you once were. So, help me understand why you're confident that you are. Because we're a people business, the only way to reconcile this is through the multiplier effect you have on other people. Unless, of course, you create a novel, proprietary idea that takes hold and produces, but how many people do that regularly?"

If you don't feel confident, then be honest with yourself and do something about it. Think about cause and effect. If the effect you want is people who are engaged, the cause of that is going to be the quality of the experience you cocreate with them. But another way of looking at cause and effect (if you want to become a little more tactical) is to play with the wording and think in terms of *causing an effect.*

I'm about to walk into a room full of people. If I go in thinking, "I have the opportunity to cause an effect, what might that look like, sound like, feel like? What would I like it to be?" That's interesting. That's something I can become more curious about.

Rather than "Why is that person looking so frustrated?" you walk in thinking, "What can I do about that? How can I shift that and shape it differently?" Instead of walking out angry or sad or disgruntled or frustrated or envious or whatever the case may be, how might they walk out feeling a little more charged up about an opportunity, a little more excited about what awaits? We often focus on what happens *to us;* but what if we focused on what happens *because of us?*

And let's not forget that the derivation of the word "deserve" is *de serve*—of service. You can only be deserving of this level of reward if your service to the world is validated accordingly. So, for all those who want to profess, "I'm deserving," OK, maybe you are, and maybe you're not. The world will always share the clues for those who are interested.

Living into the Answers

Another way of discussing *being* is calling it *presence.* When I was younger, my mother used to ask me, "Sweetheart, why are you worried?"

I'd say, "Oh, you know, Mom, I just want to do well."

And she'd say, "Just remember, worrying is focusing on what you don't want."

She was suggesting, "Don't be dismissive of something that you might temporarily call a worry, but do something

You don't have to know
if this is the best choice.
Just choose it, service it,
and see what happens.
Live into the answers.

with it." I could tell her anything I was worried about and she'd say, "So, honor that, respect it, but now tell me, how are you going to act on that?"

Ten out of ten times, that question shifts your focus from what you don't want or what you don't have to what you do want or gratitude for what you do have.

My mom followed this up with another way of looking at problems that I have taken to heart countless times. "Sweetheart, instead of putting so much pressure on yourself to somehow always have the answers, which nobody does, practice instead *living into the answers.*"

Now that is pretty much gold in my life, because it's another way of simply and clearly stating, "Be a student of your own experience." You don't have to know if this is the best choice. Just choose, give it your best, service it, and see what happens. Live into the answers—they will arise and then inform your next choice.

When Julie and I were newly married, we wondered when we would have kids and what our careers (or callings) would be and where we would live. And that expression "live into the answers" helped us find our way.

In her book *Presence* Amy Cuddy shares, "The way you carry yourself is a source of personal power—the kind of power that is the key to presence. It's the key that allows you to unlock yourself—your abilities, your creativity, your courage, and even your generosity. It doesn't give you skills or talents you don't have; it helps you to share the ones you do have. It doesn't make you smarter or better informed; it makes you more resilient and open. It doesn't change who you are; it allows you to be who you are."

MOST PEOPLE have heard the old expression "It is what it is." I like to extend that to say, "It is what it is, and it takes what it takes." At times, the only reason you may be beating yourself up is because you're asking yourself, "Why didn't I know this sooner?"

The answer is simple: "Because you didn't."

And then many say, "But, Carl, I kind of did."

I say, "Well, not to the degree necessary to consciously change your actions. But now you do know, because you've done it." So, it is what it is, and it takes what it takes. Let's be grateful for that wisdom and put it into practice, and enjoy seeing what wonderful new things are created from it.

Think of the expression "Hindsight is twenty-twenty." I also like a variation on that: "Hindsight is for fools." Most people don't like that one. But they're curious about where it comes from.

Well, everybody is perfect with hindsight. Always brilliant when looking backward. So, when I say to people, "Hindsight is for fools," I mean, "If you're going to continue to beat yourself up, no problem. I can't dissuade you from doing that, but I have one question before you carry on."

Usually people smile and say, "What's that?"

And I ask, "With all the wisdom you now have available to you, tell me in no uncertain terms, what is your next big lesson, comparable to the one you've just learned? What's it going to be? So that we don't have to wait a week or a month or a year or ten years. Go ahead, tell me what it is. You're so quick to beat yourself up over the last lesson learned, so tell me."

Of course, they can't. They have no idea. And I remind them, "And yet, just a few moments ago, you were so hard on yourself for not seeing your latest lesson sooner."

When you practice living into the answers and being a student of your own experience, you may find that you've discovered the ultimate form of agility, as long as you continue to learn along the way.

13

It's Not All
about the Money

 O
NE AFTERNOON I got two CEOs together for a meeting.
The first CEO was hoping to create some new business
opportunities with the second one, and the conversation was fantastic until about halfway through, when
the person who was looking to get more work said, "Well,
let's face it. I think we can talk candidly here as senior executives. Ultimately, we know it's all about 'show me the money.'"

As it happens, the other CEO is all about the mission,
the values, the vision, the environment, all that good stuff.
Money matters, of course, but she used to love it when I
shared, "If you consciously practice the behavior that allows
you to be the employer and supplier of choice, profit is the
applause you receive for getting it right." When I told her
that the etymology of the word "profit" is "progress," she
really loved that too. She was all about doing things for the
right reasons, for the win-win. She's a brilliant leader with
a long list of accolades. She's one of the very few people
I've known over the years who consistently role models the

best of what I've been sharing. So, when this other CEO took his "all about the money" stance because he thought it would ingratiate himself to her, she recoiled. But he was oblivious to her body language.

This carried on for a while and then I felt I had to interject. "I know you well enough to know you're joking, and that you don't believe it's all about the money. I've been around you long enough to know that you do things for these reasons…" And I proceeded to list many of the things I knew he cared about but that, for some reason, he had abandoned (my hope was temporarily).

He replied, "Oh yeah, no, for sure. Sorry. I just meant that we've got to make money to ensure longevity."

Afterward she said to me in private, "It's a good thing he had you there to clarify or I would not have offered a second meeting."

When I talked to him in the parking lot, he said, "Hey, Carl, thanks for smoothing things out a little in there. I obviously missed some cues that you picked up on."

I said, "You're very welcome. I'll leave it to you now to move forward."

Then he said, "But, Carl, come on. Every CEO knows that you follow the money."

I said, "If you believe that and it's your top priority, then I would ask, first of all, where does it say that in your company's mission statement? Or looking at your values again, where does it explicitly say that?" I was doing my best to highlight that money is an output, not an inspiring purpose or a reason for being, in and of itself.

He said, "I mean, it doesn't."

I said, "So, say what you mean and mean what you say. If your organization is going to espouse its mission, vision, and values—along with its brand promise, if you will—then why are you going down a path that is inconsistent with that?"

"But is it inconsistent?"

"Well, if I work for you because I believe in your mission and believe in the importance of living the values, and I want to get to where you say we're going regarding the vision, and then I find out that really you're just about the money, then you realize the impact that will have on me, right?"

He hesitated.

I said, "For example, why would I ever train anybody?"

"What do you mean?"

"If the only thing you, as the CEO, care about is margin and profitability, how would you feel about that being my primary focus? I'll cherry-pick the best people for my teams. I'll treat them however I want. In fact, let's be honest. They're paid fixed salaries, so the more hours I get out of them, the better; the more that drops to the bottom line."

"But why would you say, 'Why would you train?'"

I said, "Why would I train someone? That would just take away my time from cranking out cash. So, as I just suggested, I would simply cherry-pick the best people and drive them until I maximized output. If they couldn't handle it, I would go tell HR to get me someone who can. Does any of this sound familiar? You ever heard chats like this around your roundtable? I've heard some of your executives talk like that. 'If they can't handle it, get me somebody who can.' I've heard those sentiments come from your people.

"When you relegate people to widget status because it's just an assembly line to crank out output," I said, "and money is your primary objective, don't be surprised when people's behavior aligns accordingly. Becoming territorial, not willing to look out for anybody, not my job description, not on my

Choose your behavior
and you choose
your consequence.

watch—I call these Teflon managers—and notice I didn't say leaders. Nothing sticks. Finger-pointers. It's always someone else's fault. Have you ever seen that in your organization?"

He paused and then finally said, "Quite a bit, actually."

I said, "OK, well, you're the senior leader now. You didn't intend for this to be the culture, but that doesn't mean it isn't. Also recall what we've discussed before—the bridge between intention and impact is your actions. Your behaviors, your words, your tone matter. So, if you don't more consciously align your words and your actions with the intentions you declare to the market, how do you expect your brand to thrive? I'm quite sure you're not interested in a brand that projects a cutthroat 'kill or be killed' kind of culture."

I concluded with "Remember: Choose the behavior and you choose the consequence."

Fear Is (Still) Not the Answer

I talk about safety, connection, respect—but let's not kid ourselves, the number one paradigm perpetuated and reinforced in business seems to be fear-based. When leaders say, "You will get that done, right?" or "You realize what will happen if this doesn't end up the way we had planned?"—they don't realize that they're invoking fear.

I remember another CEO inviting me to sit in on a senior executive meeting about a problem one of their senior executives was having with a client. I was to observe and chime in if I heard anything that I thought might be interesting to explore. The executive in question was not going to be present. At one point, as the senior leaders were getting their coffees and catching up, I overheard them talking about the challenge, and the CEO said, "Hey, you know, but for the grace…" He didn't finish the expression, but I was familiar with how it ends, so I piped up and said, "Do you mean that?"

He said, "I beg your pardon?"

I said, "Do you mean what you just said, that but for the grace go I?"

He replied, "Yes, absolutely."

I said, "That's great to hear."

He said, "Why? Help me understand what you're getting at."

I said, "Well, that perspective is going to inform how you address this issue once the meeting starts."

"I don't follow."

"I just wanted to point out that I think it's interesting, if that perspective is fundamental to how you view this challenge."

As it turned out, it wasn't. Once the meeting was well underway, the CEO was pointing fingers, asking how this executive team could have let this happen. I knew I had to choose my timing consciously and be mindful of the team dynamic. So, on a break, I approached the CEO and asked him whether he observed any disconnect between his opening sidebar comment and how he conducted the meeting.

He very quickly, defensively ignored my question and stated, "I had to say some of the tough things that needed to be said, but that's my role."

I said, "OK, that's your role, but what about how you said these things? And since you requested that I challenge you, would you conclude that what you said and how you said it were supportive of the individual in question?"

"Oh, Carl, I think they know I support him and them."

"Well, that's not actually what I asked. What I'm asking is, did you evidence—in the words, the tone, the body language, the choices you made—support for this person, this important member of your team?"

"Did I evidence support for him? Well, he wasn't even here."

I said, "OK, on his behalf, did you set the tone that was going to encourage everybody else to want to be constructive and supportive?"

"I mean, maybe not to the extent you would have liked."

I said, "Well, it's not about me, so let me ask it differently. Do you think the team feels inspired to now rally around and support one another, that individual included? Or are they afraid and, quite frankly, just overjoyed that the spotlight was not on them?"

He said, "Well, I have no doubt they were thrilled that it wasn't them. But I'd like to think we're going to come together."

I said, "How are you helping ensure that's the case? I'm asking that very specifically. How did everything you just did and said, and how you did and said it, role model how you want the others to behave?"

He paused. "All right, I can't say I was aware of any precedent I was setting for their ongoing behavior. I guess I wasn't necessarily a role model—at least not to the extent you would have preferred."

I said, "You know what? Let's go there. Define my extent and contrast it with your extent and then help me understand, what do you think is more versus less effective?"

"Your extent, I think—and I'm giving you a lot of credit here, Carl—is to base our choices on ensuring we do what's best for the team, and adapt our body language and all these things you're talking about to be consistent with that. And I didn't pay attention to it."

"So, why didn't you?"

"I don't know."

I said, "Do you expect others to become accustomed to your leadership style instead of you focusing on their needs and adapting your style accordingly?"

He said, "Yeah, that's what every good leader does."

I paraphrased that back to him, and his smile said it all. Then I suggested that if he, as their leader, was curious, interested, and adaptive to their needs, the people he leads could carry on ensuring that the mission, vision, and values were delivered.

He said, "How can you be so sure?"

I asked if he was aware of the golden rule. He said he was and recounted, "Do unto others as you would have done unto yourself."

"What if you happen to have a particularly edgy and difficult personality, do you think most would want to be treated the way you want to be treated?"

He smiled and said, "Not likely." I suggested that this is likely why the platinum rule was invented. It states, "Do unto others as you perceive they need done unto themselves." The emphasis here being that we need to know what others need before we can best service their needs accordingly.

"So wrap this up for me, Carl: How does this relate back to my behavior during our meeting?"

"Well, you started off by suggesting that but for the grace of god you could easily have found yourself in the same situation... Is that a fair understanding about what you meant?"

"Yes, that's what the expression implies."

"OK, and yet during the meeting you behaved with very little empathy or understanding about the pressure that a team member is now facing. I would have thought that this challenge would require a focus on supportive solutions, shouldering together, and reminding the room that we're in this together—us against the issue, never against each other. Is that reasonable to suggest?"

"Yes, I get it. So, when we reconvene would it be helpful for me to hit reset, suggest we put our heads together to do everything we can to support our teammate with the best of our ideas, and encourage that we'll get through this together?"

I answered by asking if he anticipated something like this could ever happen again, to which he replied, "Of course."

I said, "There's your answer. You're literally ensuring that the team will now appreciate the way you expect all future such issues be handled. You're influencing constructively while bringing out everyone's level best. That sounds like leadership to me."

Authenticity, Adaptability, Empathy

During the same session, the CEO asked me, "What's the number one mistake most leaders make, in your estimation?"

I said, "Thinking that they must have all the answers. They don't realize that their responsibility is to build teams whose members complement one another's diverse strengths and then, together, cocreate the best answers in service of a mission that matters." Not to mention, most answers don't even exist yet. If you pretend to be the one who always has the answers, you paint yourself into a corner and are proven wrong (or inconsistent) regularly, thus eroding trust along the way.

I added, "Harvard once did this research piece that said three things more than anything else will determine your effectiveness as a leader. The first is your willingness to acknowledge a mistake, because that speaks to your authenticity. The second is your willingness to acknowledge when you don't know something, because that speaks to your adaptability. The third is whether you are inclined to understand someone else before needing to be understood yourself, because that speaks to your empathy. If you just looked at those three—authenticity, adaptability, and empathy—and the way Harvard described them, how do you think you fared?"

"Yeah, OK, you got me. I never acknowledge being wrong."

I said with a smile, "Correct me if I'm wrong, but maybe you also have yet to make your first mistake."

He said, "I get it. Thanks, Carl."

We were at a stage in our relationship where we could have some fun with this and make it meaningful at the same time. The release of pressure that otherwise accompanies the expectation of having all the answers is a tremendous upside.

I asked him, "Why do you think a leader who is willing to acknowledge not having the answers or who admits to making mistakes is helpful to their followers?"

He paused and then said, "Because it makes them human."

"How so?"

"They can conclude that they too don't need to know everything and can acknowledge making a mistake."

"I love that, yes. And how important do you think that is to business—be it in relation to risk management, innovation, team performance, or effective communication?"

His final thought: "Critical!" We smiled, shook hands, hugged, and left for a friendly dinner together. It had been a very interesting and instructive day.

Welcome to Life in a Fishbowl

Once I went to a town hall where a CEO was speaking and wanted me to observe and provide feedback. His smile was the first thing I noticed when he took the stage. Perhaps because I rarely saw him smile. Then came the excitement in his voice; the conviction of his organization's purpose was evident in his words. He conveyed a positivity and a clear sense of gratitude for all those in attendance. He used humor repeatedly (and effectively), took questions while looking

What would the
best version of you
do or say?

intently at the individuals asking them, and answered with care, compassion, and transparency. He led the applause for others who would later share the stage and made it clear that together they were better and projected his excitement for the future that they could (and would) cocreate together. Inspired and inspiring.

He approached me afterward and said, "So?"

I said, "Tell me, would the average person in this organization conclude that you are, behind closed doors, the very essence of what they just witnessed on stage?"

"I'd like to think so."

"OK, that's nice, but what does your observed track record tell you?"

"I think you're asking me this question because you've heard things about me."

"Well, sure. We hear things about lots of people."

"My guess is what you've heard doesn't align with what you saw on stage."

Yet again, I asked a senior leader a neutral question and his intuition was telling him he had a misalignment. In this case, he suspected his public persona differed from the experience of him in private. Sometimes people go there because they're their own worst critic. I get that. But this wasn't the case. He knew he didn't behave in public the way he does behind closed doors, and furthermore, he knew he leveraged fear more than he might care to admit. He kept his eyes on me, while I watched him think. Finally he said, "I'm not sure why."

"OK, so if you could practice more consciously being the person you are on stage, everywhere, would that be worthwhile?"

"If I think about why I bring that level of energy, openness, and enthusiasm to the stage in the first place, that's my answer. If I became more proficient at being the same person and leader everywhere I go, it would lend itself to fewer surprises, safer spaces, and higher quality conversations." He asked if other CEOs I work with do a better job of this, and if so, how they did it.

"Regarding the first part of your question, I don't think that's relevant," I replied. "What's relevant is whether you're interested in being a little better and more effective today than you were yesterday. And we both know your answer to this."

As for the second part, I smiled and shared how another CEO once said of his role, "Welcome to life in a fishbowl." He understood that the spotlight comes with the territory—everywhere, in every instance and venue. Everybody's looking, everybody can see you, and often they want to. You're always on. Get used to it and recognize the responsibility that comes with that. The possibility of influencing and cocreating an incredibly positive ripple effect becomes priority number one; but without conscious intention and consistent practice, many produce a toxic ripple instead. If a leader does not embrace this understanding, or finds it too much to handle, then this is not the role for them.

This point is relevant to all of us, regardless of our position. How do you behave when others aren't watching? If you knew they were watching, would you behave differently? What would the best version of you do or say?

Naturally, we'll all continue to make mistakes. Just remember that acknowledging mistakes gives others permission to do the same. Fostering deeper, more authentic, and meaningful relationships will be the result—relationships where common humanity is at the center of all you say and do. No one ever has been perfect, and you and I will not be the first. Understanding this contributes to a level of humility conducive to resonant relationships that build trust and a safe space to explore, experiment, and grow.

14

Remind Me, Why Compassionate Action?

S TARTING WITH compassion comes in handy for another critical reason. There's only one reason why anyone is difficult to deal with: It seems to always be in relation to an insecurity. What they are insecure about may never be anyone's business, but you can take this insight to the bank.

How do we know? Well, imagine for a moment that you have the mindset of someone who understands and appreciates that you are already whole. You're an original, you're enough, and your only responsibility in life is to contribute the best of who you are in service of this moment. With this in mind, tell me, to retain this mindset would you ever need to belittle someone or hold yourself out as superior in some way? Do you need others to feel lesser about themselves for you to remain whole in who you are?

I have asked this question countless times and everyone understands (quickly) that the answer is no. So, if you find yourself needing to compare, judge, and/or focus on defending a position, whatever it may be, just know that this stems from some underlying insecurity. We would never behave this way from a position of strength. Sure, results may vary, and there will be times when you may not attain a specific goal—but whether you succeed or not will have no bearing on who you are. And on the deepest level, you know this.

Why do I share this? Because, now that we understand the important role compassion plays in our overall health and well-being, we can remain compassionate in the face of a difficult situation or person. If it proves true within your own experience that the main reason for someone behaving in a difficult manner stems from an insecurity, you can remain compassionate and focused on creating a solution despite the current challenges. Let's see what that could look like.

You Can't Tear a Strip off Me

If every time you encounter uncertainty, you perceive it as a threat, then when someone destabilizes you, you go into fight-or-flight or you freeze or faint. Your cells constrict, your nervous system shuts down, and you think you've got to survive.

Imagine you come into my office and close the door and proceed to yell at me—attempt to "tear a strip off me." I choose those words very consciously, because as I often say, "You can't actually tear a strip off me without my permission."

When someone tries to tear a strip off me, there is one of two possibilities. Either I was involved in the thing they're yelling at me about or I wasn't. If I was involved, then first of all, I care about you, I like you, I respect you. That alone, contextually speaking, means the last thing I would ever want to do, truthfully in my heart of hearts, is to be the cause of

Practice being conscious of your own intention.

anything that would put you in this state. So, my very humble and sincere response to someone would be "Hey, first of all, Ron, I want you to know that I was involved in the thing you're talking about."

And Ron might say, "Yeah, no kidding, Carl. Why do you think I'm here?"

"Well, I'm only pointing that out because very often that's not the case. I wanted you to know that I was involved. But I also want you to know that it kind of tears me up to think that I contributed to something that would have you encounter this kind of an experience, so I might have a few questions to ask. But I assure you I will do everything in my power to rectify this, resolve it, and get more information. I hope you're OK with that, but I'm here with you and for you, and I am just so sorry that this has happened."

This is not about magically thinking that everything will now be fine. But let me ask you, do you think that Ron's blood pressure would at least hold its current level?

I'm calming him down, so absolutely it would. Most people drop down a level and share, "You know what, you're right. We're a team. I know you didn't do it on purpose. Sorry I was so harsh and thank you..."

And that's if I *was* involved. If I wasn't involved, which is most of the time (usually people yell at others because of things that don't even involve them—wrong place, wrong time), my response would have been something like, "Hey, Ron, first of all, thanks for coming to see me because you know we respect each other as colleagues. Second of all, I really appreciate that you closed the door [said with a smile on my face]. Thirdly, you need to know that I wasn't involved in what you're talking about. However, go ahead and vent. Get it off your chest. Let it go, and then just know that I'm here with you and for you, to help you figure something out now." Always us against the issue, never against each other.

Of course, then a person drops even quicker and says something like, "Oh, I thought you were involved. Do you know..."

My point is, when you practice being conscious of your own intention, you can walk into every interaction knowing you'll give your best. You won't take shortcuts or try to manipulate someone or try to beat them at a game. And when you practice that, it's far more likely that you'll remain centered in the face of any kind of situation, because you will be looking for the solution rather than to defend or to blame or to deflect. That does wonders for your ability to positively influence.

Remaining compassionate allows you to access the best of your thinking (regardless of what's happening outside yourself). This knowledge can help center you even under challenging external circumstances.

Finally, for everything you do for others, consider doing it equally for yourself. In other words, yes, it's wonderful to convey compassion for others... just please practice being as compassionate with yourself.

15

Authenticity and Identity

P EOPLE OFTEN say to me, "Carl, so much of what we're talking about is having a profound impact on my personal life, not just my professional life." A lot of these people realize that being the same person everywhere they go in their lives can be efficient and effective. I see many people who are completely different in front of their family than they are in the workplace. A lot of science supports the idea that you're far better off being the same person everywhere you go. The nature of your responsibilities may be different, but the essence (and energy) that is you is the same regardless of the role.

This reminds me of a discussion I once had with the most senior female partner at a local law firm. Let's call her Jane. She asked if I could help her because she was dealing with too much fallout from her leadership style.

I said, "I've been privileged enough to be invited to your home; my family and your family have spent quality time together. We've had many conversations in which you are candid and open and constructive about your business and excited about its future." Then I added, "Why do you think others in your firm have not had the benefit of seeing you in that light?"

She replied, "I have no idea."

I said, "Well, only you will know the truth about this. My experience of you is that you're the same person with me all the time. But my sense from what you've shared is that others don't experience you that way. Meaning you're a different person with certain individuals. Is it possible that's true?"

Jane replied, "Meaning direct to a fault, command-oriented, dismissive, difficult?" She started to tear up.

I closed her door and said, "You know if there's anything I can do to support you . . ." and then next thing you know she confided in me that she had been receiving some coaching from senior partners, all men, who were saying she had to behave that way if she wanted to make it. Basically, the nurturing side of her would get chewed up and taken advantage of.

I said, "I'm here to tell you that the opposite is my experience." Many people at her previous firm knew her to be a nurturing person who celebrated birthdays, ensured gifts were arranged for special occasions, gave heartfelt handwritten cards, and remembered many a family member by name. I told her, "People need more of that person, both as their leader and as someone who evidences care and compassion."

She told me she cried because she had been betraying who she wanted to be (and who she knew herself to be). She had been pretending to be someone she wasn't.

I said, "Well, you're going to have to choose which version of you shows up. But I will say this: Many people will not stay here if the version of you that shows up, day in and day out, is not the real you. Unless you think you're a good enough actor to keep track of multiple personas?"

She said, "No, thank you for that wake-up call, Carl." And we proceeded to team together for many years. She found the courage to stay true to herself, practiced being the same person everywhere she went, and—imagine that—became an office favorite who went on to many rewarding senior leadership roles.

Being the Source of What You Seek

Another senior partner at a different firm, Alice, had been a trailblazer for women in senior positions in law firms. We had developed a terrific relationship through our charity work in the community; she had also made time to get to know my family as well. I remember visiting her office once, enjoying our chat, when she abruptly said, "Carl, please close my door."

Alice said, "I have a question for you, and it's going to sound very unorthodox but it's genuine."

I said OK, and she said, "How is it that you never let me get away with being difficult?" I laughed, and she continued, "See what I mean? You laugh at a moment like this. You just don't let me get away with it!"

I said, "Because you're not difficult."

"Well, maybe not with you, but I can't quite figure out why that is."

We talked about the kind of things I spoke about with Jane, and she eventually said, "You know what it is? I sense that many men around here treat me as the token skirt. I meet certain quotas for this or that. Whereas you respect me and treat me like you do everyone else, *and* you're willing to be honest with me. That allows me to drop my barriers and just be more of who I am with you."

I said, "Well, isn't that wonderful."

"What do you mean?"

I said, "Everything we do with one another is an attempt, hopefully, to create an environment where everybody ultimately gives themselves permission to be who they are, in service of something that matters to them, in a way that aligns with their strengths, because then it's a win-win-win, right? So, isn't that wonderful!"

She replied, "So, how do I do that?"

"It's simple—you just decide that you're going to be you, no matter what comes your way."

"OK, can you help me to do that?"

"Sure."

"Because you're somebody who, anytime I get really angry or whatever, you just call me on it in a supportive way. And I'm just grateful to you for that." And she gave me a big hug.

As we wrapped up this conversation, Alice asked if I had any quick tips for where to start. I said, "Practice being the source of what you seek. Think about all the ways you want to positively impact people, and ideally how you would like them to respond to you. With that in mind, start behaving that way yourself, rather than waiting for others to take the lead. I suggest you'll find that you get what you give. If you lead with kindness, you'll attract more of the same. If you concentrate on being a terrific listener, others will feel compelled to listen more attentively to you." With a smile, I concluded, "If you want others to be fascinated by you, and who wouldn't, practice being fascinated by them."

How to Be the Author of Your Authentic Identity

Both Jane and Alice learned to stop pretending and instead be who they really are. So, how can you be authentic?

What are your top virtues? You can choose values and put them into practice. Ask yourself which values you want to operationalize into virtues.

Etymologies can be so informative. The root of "authenticity" is "author." Being authentic is about authoring your own life experience so that you can positively impact others. If you're going to author, will something emanate from you, or will you always write about someone else? And by the way, nobody knows you better than you, so why wouldn't you tell us your story, if there's one to be told? Which there always is.

Which brings us to the question, what is identity? The root of "identity" is "consistency of beingness." I absolutely love that because it suggests curiosity about what it is like to be in your presence, more often than not. We don't necessarily think about that or make a conscious competence out of it. We don't necessarily ask about the effect the experience that we are cocreating with another has on us both.

Everybody reading this has an identity. The experience of being in your presence from one moment to the next has some consistency. That's your identity. Your identity—your current-state identity, if you will—is how others experience you. It is probably also how you perceive yourself—though how you perceive yourself and how others perceive you are not always aligned. That's one thing to keep in mind.

So, you've got a current-state identity. And you also have the art of the possible at your disposal. Who would you describe yourself to be at your very best? What would a future vision of your best self look like?

Why is that important? Because if you've got an idea of what you look like and how you are being experienced today along with an idea of what the best version of you looks like, then you can have a lot of fun closing the gap between who you currently are and who you are capable of being. That's why identity can be so instructive, and also why the word derives from "consistency of beingness."

The more regularly you behave in a particular way because it relates to the best version of yourself, the more likely it is that those around you will experience you accordingly. Notice what that does. It allows you to author your identity by design, rather than by mere chance.

So, how do you choose your best-self identity? There are two ways.

Firstly, there's static identity. You could say, for example, "I want to be like a gold-medal Olympian." This is a static identity that relates to a future vision, which can be highly instructive. Because if you take it on, then for any word you utter, any action you take, any experience you cocreate with someone else, you can ask yourself, "Is this what the gold-medal Olympian in me would do and say in this moment?" You can choose based on what that future identity—that gold-medal version of yourself—would do, rather than defaulting to the current state. When it comes to static identities, though, we can be pretty tough on ourselves. When you make a decision that does not align with that gold-medal Olympic version of yourself, you might be harsh and judgmental. When you judge, you resist. This often becomes a persistent cycle.

That's why I'm partial to what I call a dynamic identity, which comes from asking, "Who am I at my best, and how can I portray that moment to moment?"

For instance, when thinking about the *quality* of my energy, I might choose a dynamic identity aligned with being a radiant exemplar. With everything I do, I could practice being mindful about whether I felt a radiance, an authenticity, an originality, an exuberance, an enthusiasm about just being me. And the second half of that is "Am I being exemplary?" I might look back on each experience to assess whether my kids or friends or colleagues would say, "You know what, you were an exemplar in that instance."

If I were to look at the *focus* of my energy, I might choose to be a loving optimalist. "Loving" because, to me, everything is about loving, and then do as you will. The "optimalist" is about being accepting of the world, which can (and will) create constraints—the challenges of humanity remind us of this all the time. Life happens and it can be hard. But when whatever it is comes my way, can I respond in an optimal way? The optimalist considers the current constraints and then does the very best possible in service of that moment.

If I also chose a dynamic identity for the *expression* of my energy, my aspirational identity might be that of an encouraging essence. "Encouraging" because we can all use some encouragement, and "essence" to remind me of our loving nature when free of fear, and my desire to influence others positively.

Designing Your Identity

What will help you tap the full potential of your identity? Intention.

How can you develop your identity today, by design, in the same ways that a company builds its brand?

You are limited only by your imagination. For example, in addressing the focus of your energy, if you are an athlete, you may want to identify as an athlete when it comes to your health. And maybe in the workplace, you want to identify as a leader (as opposed to, for example, a victim). If I want the leader in me to be present more often than the victim, no matter what comes my way, I ask myself, "What would the leader in me do next? What would the leader in me say now?"

That in and of itself can be instructive. My next question is, what virtues do you think most resonate with you and that future best version of yourself, who is a leader in any given circumstance?

And why did I say "virtues"? Most of us in the corporate world tend to talk in terms of values—which is fantastic, by the way. Values are aspirational in nature; they're future-state, hopeful ways of behaving. Virtues are actualized values. So, when you hear someone talking about someone else as virtuous, it means that they put their values into action. So, if you identify as a leader, what are your top two or three virtues? You can choose values, but I want you to put them into practice, because the bridge from theory to mastery is practice. You've got to do something to evolve toward the identity you revere. So, start with identity, then ask yourself which top values you want to operationalize and so turn into virtues.

When you choose a behavior, you choose a consequence. When you start with identity, you start with the end in mind. I've got an idea of who I am at my best, and I understand what virtues align with that identity. Now I can give more conscious thought to the behaviors that will exemplify those virtues. With consistent practice, my new habits will take hold and, before long, move me from where I am currently to who I am at my best.

I WAS GIVING a talk once and someone asked, "Doesn't my past always dictate my future?" My response was "No, unless you choose to not change any of your behaviors." And the whole place burst out laughing. I added, "In which case, I can assure you, your future will be exactly like your past."

In your daily life, when you are on the receiving end of a heartfelt thanks, that is a sign of your genius.

If you practice being more conscious of a behavior, if you are more intentional about where you place your attention, you'll find your good intentions manifest more consciously, by design. That creates a consistency, which then revamps your identity. It precedes you, so that in any relationship going forward, people will already have a sense of who you are—your actions will have already evidenced that to them.

This applies to companies too. When I'm invited to talk to one, I often start by saying, "By the way, Company X, when I research you and your website and I look at your mission, vision, and values, I already know what I expect this experience is going to be like. Do you know that's my expectation, and do you think that expectation is fair?"

People always say that yes, it's fair, but the observation terrifies them.

Play to Your Interests and Your Strengths

A lot of research out there looks at how important it is to play to your interests and your strengths. Often the world around us will let us know what our strengths are. An exercise you can do is to reflect on when people around you tend to give you the most heartfelt thanks. I don't mean a passing "thanks, friend, see you again." I mean those moments where someone says, "Hey, do you have a minute? I want you to know that what you did for me in that moment was so instructive, [or so inspirational, so life-changing] that if you had not made the time for me, I hazard to think what I would have missed and the benefits foregone! So, thank you." In your daily life, when is it that people around you—from mere acquaintances to loved ones or colleagues and coworkers—give you those moments of heartfelt thanks?

Why do I ask that? Because when you are on the receiving end of a heartfelt thanks, that is a sign of your genius. That is when your authenticity—the author of you—is at its best, in the most prevalent way. The world wants to mirror that; it wants to give as it receives. Be mindful of that, because where those heartfelt thank-yous intersect with what interests you is where your innate strengths tend to reside.

If you do that reflective exercise, you'll probably have an easier time finding a few words to describe the essence of who you are when you are at your best. When you choose that identity and then practice a level of awareness as you make decisions that you think align with that identity, what responses are people giving you? Very often we're not mindful of that. We go in and out of our days, people say and do things, and we're not conscious of the quality of the experience we cocreate with them.

The greater your level of awareness, the greater your ability to self-regulate and lead toward choices that align with that best version of yourself. That slowly closes the gap between who you know yourself to be today and who you know you're capable of being, which is the beauty of understanding identity. Because if you begin with the end in mind—"here's who I think I can be at my best"—and use that vision of yourself to drive your decisions, then that bodes well for you and for those around you. Being intentional about your identity feeds mindful next steps and, practiced regularly, will help you manifest your best.

Choosing a Positive Identity

Be conscious not to choose an identity that the world imposes on you. The key tool is your intuition—your inner teacher. Once in a while, ask yourself (rather than everyone else) who you could be. Research by Richard Boyatzis and others says that if your identity aligns with your "ought self"—as in, you ought to do this or ought to be that—then your life will revolve around "shoulds." And as you've heard others say, we need to stop "shoulding" on ourselves. The second you hear someone say "should have done"—yeah, wonderful, but that's not what happened.

What's going to be more instructive? That ideal version from within. The one where you're using your own experience. Where are you at your best? Where do people want to thank you in a heartfelt way because of the impact you're having on them? The truer you are to that, the more inclined you'll be to author your own path.

For example, if "creator" is your chosen identity, that is nice because we're designed to grow and expand and nurture the quality of evolving. What might be a contrasting identity? Victim. Imagine you have two choices for your aspirational identity: creator or victim. When life happens and things come your way, the victim in you would say, "Woe is me. I can't believe this is happening to me again. Can I tell you about it, friend?" Misery loves company. And what happens to who you can be at your best? Nothing. Because it's all about what's happening *to* you and convincing yourself that you have no control. You've given up your control and your authenticity, and consequently (so you think) your ability to do or say otherwise.

In contrast, imagine your identity is of a creator. That means every time life comes your way, you respond to it reflectively—rather than react, like the victim—by saying, "OK, so it is what it is. How do I cocreate something out of this moment that can be helpful to both you and me?"

That's what I mean about always playing to the win-win. I would never sacrifice a colleague for my benefit, nor would they ever allow me to sacrifice myself for their benefit, and the creator would never go there because they would be looking at, first, what is happening here, and second, how do we create something anew? How do we manifest a different reality that can serve everyone involved more effectively? Notice the difference between the creator in me and the victim in me. Anyone can practice these things, and you must practice if you want to see (and experience) the difference.

So, why would you choose an identity that is not going to serve you or those around you most effectively? You wouldn't. But don't leave this to chance. We all know how often we assume the role of the victim because we aren't more intentional about who we want to be. So, be intentional about being a creator throughout your day today.

Notice one more difference between the creator and the victim. The creator focuses on what can emanate from you and through you in service of another and the moment, whereas the victim is focused on what happens to you—no growth, no expansion, no progression.

And we've come full circle, back to the consistency of beingness.

If you want to be more intentional, more by design, more aligned with who you can be at your best, why wouldn't you give some thought to what that would look like? Is it common that people do this? No. Statistically, only about 3 percent of individuals reading this have ever overtly done an exercise that identifies their top one or two or three personal values (let alone the identity these values serve). Which means, sure, we're all good people and well-intentioned (one would hope!), but how conscious are we of our intentions? If we're not conscious of our values or what we want to be intentional about, then we are leaving it to chance.

The Gap between Who You Are and Who You Say You Are

My friend Sandy is a behavioral neuroscientist. When she finished her maternity leave, after having been gone from her office for a year, on day one, she opened her laptop, sat down, and thought, "Well, let's see what's changed since I was last here."

We had talked a lot during her time off, had lots of fun discussing her specialty (she has a PhD in that space). She said, "You know what, Carl? I'm going to make sure that I am a student of my own experience, as you often suggest." On the first day back at the office, with a smile on her face, she listened to what she had missed, to the latest mandates, to what was required of her (and by when), to the new pressures she was expected to navigate (seemingly on her own), and to what had happened to the team in her absence. All that stuff. Then she closed her laptop, smiled, and went home and told her husband, "Guess what? I'm done. I'm not going to pretend anymore."

The truth is, her return wasn't a welcoming experience. It wasn't "We missed you. We're so excited. We can't wait to hear what you have to say about this." It wasn't, by any means, "Don't worry, we're going to support you and here's how." Daniel Siegel often discusses attachment theory, which has to do with the type of attachments that relationships can offer. When relationships are good for our health and our ability to perform well, they consist of the four *s*'s: seeing, soothing, safety, and security. When we see someone soothing any concerns and creating safety, it leads to a sense of security. Sandy had a lot on her mind returning to the office, where she was not seen and no one attempted to empathize with her concerns nor tried to create a sense of safety and security for her. The result was a lack of belonging. We all want to belong, and she felt that she no longer did.

"What had changed since the last time you were there?" I asked. She shared that while she was away, she logged in regularly and stayed on top of everything senior leadership said in their town halls. She noted the key messages, about what they said of their values and who they were. But when she returned from maternity leave, Sandy felt the misalignment and just shook her head. She started looking for opportunities with other organizations.

Sandy became a senior leader at a global Fortune 100 company. During the interview, they celebrated her vision and how empathic she was; then they went away and created the role of a lifetime for her. I talked to her the other day and she said, "Oh my gosh, Carl, it's unbelievable. And this would never have happened if I hadn't trusted in myself. I've often heard it said that when someone shows you who they are, believe them. I'm so grateful that I did just that."

What does it say about the corporate world today that more than a few leaders have no conscious competence around their identity, no awareness of what it's like to be in their presence? I like to ask leaders, "Which top three words would others use to describe you if you weren't in the room? If those three words resonate with you, align with your aspirations, your greatest version of yourself, awesome, love it!

Did you do that by design? How are you going to make sure you sustain that?"

But many are a little uneasy about that question. "I'm not sure what people would say. I'm not sure how consistent it would be..." That means that their identity is far more by chance than by design. As leaders, we can all be better than that.

16

Play and Have Fun

_____

T O RETURN to sport, coaches will say to athletes, "Just go out there and have fun." Sometimes people feel that rules are restrictive, but have you ever played tennis without a court or a net? The game is much better with them. And as soon as you say, "Let's start keeping score," it's a whole new level. It can be so much fun, *not* because someone loses but because when you embrace the competition, you get a feel for just how good you can be. It gives you a baseline against which you can measure progress, and we are designed to evolve. We, as energy, are made to evidence growth and expansiveness. Energy expands.

Even balance is dynamic. Look at tightrope walkers. Balancing on a tightrope is not a static event; it's highly active. They're constantly in motion because movement provides balance. Life rewards action and dynamism when you're playful. Watch children at a playground, and then look at people who are playful and see what they do. Look at their level of creativity—the boundless nature of it, the color palettes they pick, the strength they somehow find.

My kids were watching *American Idol* the other day and Derek Hough, a professional dancer, was coaching some singers. He was talking about stage presence and he used a line I love: "You don't *have* confidence; you *do* confidence." I talked to them about that afterward. I said the etymology of the word "confidence" is "intense trust"—in your ability to serve and contribute meaningfully. And the best way to cultivate confidence is to do what you say you'll do. So, if you tell me you'll meet me at 1 p.m. and we meet at 1 p.m., you've just bolstered your trust in yourself, even if you're not aware of it. Over time, you cultivate confidence because you realize that you have trust and agency over yourself. When you constantly cancel, I still might like you, absolutely love you even, but I probably won't trust you to meet me. You're just not reliable enough. Trust, not surprisingly, is about credibility (your words), reliability (your actions), and transparency (your emotional intelligence). Be mindful of how your choices reflect your credible, reliable, emotionally intelligent best, in service of someone else's needs—and watch the trust grow, while having fun along the way.

Inputs, Outputs, and Outcomes

I was talking to a sports physiologist who had some nuanced things to say about outcome versus output. He was warning athletes not to focus on the outcome—the gold medal, the trophy—because it involves a whole lot of things they can't control, such as the competition or a referee's call, the weather, sheer bad luck, a rogue bounce leading to a goal. Instead he coached his athletes to concentrate on the output, the thing they can control—how well they perform. If they do everything they can to the best of their abilities, the accolades will follow.

Even if you don't win, knowing you've done your best, from your authentic self, has a magic attached to it. Because rather than living from a place of mere thinking, you become one of the few who live from a place of knowing.

I also like that when people think of output, they automatically think of input. And of course, the quality of your inputs will directly determine the quality of your outputs. So, what are the quality of your inputs? That question relates to your energy: the quality of it, the focus of it, the expression of it. Not to mention physical inputs of nutrition, sleep, movement, breathing. If you make a habit out of enhancing those inputs, you can't help but elevate the quality of your output. And again you don't need to believe me or the physiologists when we say that. You can just nuance an aspect of your sleep, nutrition, movement, and so on, and ask yourself how you feel as a result of that one change. You can act your way into believing.

WHEN I was younger, my dad once said to me, "Hey, Carl, I'm curious. Do you think you get your joy from what you do, or rather do you practice bringing joy to what you do? Which one do you think will serve you and everyone else best?"

I replied, "Oh, man, well, I know what I want to say, but that's interesting."

"Tell me more. Why is it interesting?"

"Because the world would have me believe that there is some vocation, some task, some destination, some outcome, where joy-filled experience would reside in every moment. And yet if I practice bringing my joy to what I do instead, I will probably find that joy made manifest."

And my dad said, "Interesting. Well, maybe experiment with that and see how it works for you and those you're with."

I did just that, and the choice became crystal clear. I hope you have fun running the same experiment.

Living for the Experience—and for the Joy of It

One day early in my coaching career, I had the honor and good luck to work at a charity event with a famous athlete of our time, an Olympic champion. We were chatting and she started talking about her early days, when she had a coach and a support system who all believed that the point of competing was winning, and only winning. She convinced herself of this too and was willing to put her body through whatever it took to prove she was the best. After years of struggle, she finally won her first world championship, at last proving to the whole world that she was the indisputable best in her field.

The next morning, she was sitting with her mom in a café enjoying a celebratory cappuccino when she broke down in tears. Her mother sat quietly, allowing the emotion to flow. When the tears started to slow, she took her daughter's hand and said, "When you're ready, dear, I'm happy to listen if you would like to share what's on your mind." It was a sweet moment, but the athlete's emotions were still hijacking her, so the pair sat quietly for a while to allow her thoughts to crystallize.

She eventually turned to her mother and said, "Mom, I'm not any different!"

To which her mother replied, "Of course you're not, dear, you're the same lovable person you've always been."

"No, Mom, you don't understand. I'm supposed to be different. Winning the world championship was supposed to

You, as energy, are
made to evidence growth
and expansiveness.
Energy expands.

make me whole, complete, content... I don't know how to express it... but I was supposed to feel different!"

This was a wake-up call. She had been so consumed with the destination that she never focused on enjoying the journey. Once the lights and cameras were turned off, and everyone else was moving on with their lives, all that seemed to remain was an emptiness where she had expected something else. "I don't know what exactly," she joked with me. "Maybe for the clouds to part and angels to start singing?" Instead, there was only silence in a small café in a foreign land.

This epiphany changed her. She finally understood what it truly meant to prioritize the journey and not the destination. Our life itself is contained within each step of the journey; the destination is just some future date on the calendar.

Not only did she carry on in her sport, but she dominated it. She became holistically healthy for the first time in her life and her results reflected that. Win or lose, she focused on having fun, loving the challenge, owning her chosen path, and soaking in every second, because the time was always now. For the first time in her life, she really understood this.

When she finished telling me this story, I thanked her and encouraged her to please share it with others—it was too good and too important to keep to herself. So many people that know and love her would be thrilled to hear these kinds of insights that put things into the proper perspective. She said, "Thank you, Carl. I may choose to share one day but until then it will be our secret."

I smiled and said, "I can't promise I won't share it—it's too good to keep to myself. But I promise I won't mention any names." I still think it best to leave that to her.

With a hug and a smile, she said, "Deal!"

17

Relationships
Are Everything

A T A recent conference, some folks were talking about how relationships are everything, and they asked me if I had any examples to make that sentiment real. I said, "Absolutely."

To give you some context, during the three days of this conference, I was with the senior leaders of a multinational organization. On the second evening, they were hosting a gala reception at a local hotspot. They invited some of the younger people from the company, to give them a chance to get to know some of their senior leaders.

I found the younger folks highly receptive and happy to be there. They gathered in groups and they had tons of questions. At one point, they were saying, "You know, everyone always says relationships are everything. Can you give us a practical example of that?"

I smiled and replied, "Where are you in your career?" They told me they were new managers.

I said, "I can remember like yesterday being a new manager in a similar firm to the one you're in. And believe it or not, once in a blue moon I was asked to work late." Of course, they all laughed. I added, "Right, it was all the time!"

I told them that I'd met my wife in second-year university and we'd been together for many years when I became a manager. In fact, Julie and I were already married by that time. So, whenever I was asked to work late, I would give her a call, which would usually sound something like "Hey, Jules, how was your day? This was my day and, by the way, I've been asked if I can work late." And Julie always gave the same response, without exception.

These young folks looked at me smiling, like, "What did she say?"

"She would say, 'Who's asking?'"

If it was these names on the left, then she would say, "Oh, that's fantastic, say hi to them for me, and can I do anything for you, maybe pick up some food and drop it off at the office?"

But if it was these names on the right, she would say, "No, sorry, you've got commitments at home. I need you here."

These young folks were laughing and saying, "Wow."

And I said, "So, would you like to know what constituted being on the left-hand list versus the right-hand list?" They were eager to hear.

Julie's response was simple but profound, and she is a fair person; she is not judgmental and is super easygoing. She is also very astute and observant, and she realized that, of all the people we'd met at many social events, certain leaders always went out of their way to find us in the crowd. To thank me for what I had been doing, to thank Julie for my time, to thank her for her support of me—because clearly they knew that once in a while I'd been asked to work longer than was ideal. They'd tell her "how great Carl has been for us, and we don't know what we would do without him," and so on.

The individuals on the right-hand list had the same opportunity. We would see them and talk to them, but they didn't express gratitude or appreciation. The talk was more superficial: "Nice to meet you." "Goodbye." Julie thought that was fascinating, given that these were the senior leaders. These were people who could celebrate progress and camaraderie along with the life energy that a person invested for the benefit of their business. It was never lost on her that these individuals seemed to care more about themselves than the people who were helping them drive the success of the organization. They all had equal opportunity, but the names on the left-hand side decided to invest, to celebrate, to be grateful, to show appreciation—and the names on the right never did.

"So," I said, "the moral of this story is, which list are you on? And which one do you aspire to be on? Are you mindful of the experience that you're cocreating with all the people in your midst? You are new managers early on in your careers, but you have people who report to you. Have you given much thought to whether those people want to follow you?"

The best followers are the ones who want to follow. In other words, lead like everyone is a volunteer, and see who gravitates toward you because they're inspired to. Not because it's politically convenient or because you have formal authority, or whatever else the case may be.

The young managers stood there and said, "I'm sure we can do better at this."

THE NEXT morning at one of the sessions, a few people asked, "Hey, Carl, I saw a group of young people listening to you. What were you talking about?"

I summarized what I had said, and asked, "What do you hear when I share that?"

Playfulness, hopefulness, compassion, and mindfulness are the four modes of operation that put you in the state to access your best.

One individual raised their hand and said, "I have to tell you, I'm hoping last night was an exception because so many of us are new with each other, so we wanted to get to know each other as senior leaders."

Another said, "You know, I didn't go out of my way to talk to any of the junior people there. I'm not a bad person. It just wasn't my intention. I was focused more on trying to get to know some of my peers."

I replied, "In fairness to you, this was the first time you've ever had a conference like this, and you are trying to get to know each other as well. But next time around, if you already know the senior people in the room, just ask yourself how intentional you are about going out of your way to not just meet the younger managers but to evidence your appreciation for those who show up, day in and day out, for your benefit and the benefit of the clients you all serve."

Julie's litmus test was always funny to me. She would always ask that same question of me, and it wasn't until the third or fourth time that I said, "When are you going to tell me more about what you're thinking?"

And she replied, "Carl, I'm supportive of the ones who are supportive of you. We've always said that we get what we give in life, but don't give to get. And I'm sure when we have kids one day we'll teach them that." Which we did. For her, it was so straightforward.

People are often called on to put in more time for the workplace. The people with more formal authority who decide to celebrate an entire family for their support of a team member's time will always fare better than those who show little regard. That's just the way it is.

At that same conference, we were talking about choice and some people asked, "Do we really have a choice?" I thought to myself, "Well, change is a constant, and principles are too, so in theory, all you have to do is make principle-based choices in the face of never-ending change and you're good." That's tougher than it sounds, though, because our emotions often get in the way. But it's worth practicing anyway.

Saying No

Not long after I became a senior manager, a partner sat down in my office one day. "Carl," he said, "I'm so excited. You and I have never had a chance to work together. And this massive opportunity just landed on my desk and I thought now's the time, I have to get Carl involved. So here's the deal..." He told me about the project, the client, and his excitement to work together.

I looked at him and said, "First of all, thank you so much for thinking of me. Second of all, thank you for thinking of me in the way that you've just articulated. I'm going to need a bit of time to check this opportunity against my existing scheduled commitments. And I might need your help, because at the current moment I'm not sure that I'll be able to say yes, with everything else the way it stands."

He looked back at me and said, "Are you saying no to me?"

I said, "I mean, I don't want to put it that way. I'm saying that I'm not sure I can responsibly say yes to something new of this scale given everything else I've already committed to. Out of fairness to my previous yeses, I need to take a hard look at what I would need and circle back around with some of the scheduling. And I'm going to need to responsibly talk to some of the other partners who I'm working with to let them know of this big project. We might need their collective input, that's all."

He became audibly and visibly upset with me. His tone of voice, his word choices, his body language all gave me clues. He was making my response personal and emotional. He stood, clearly frustrated, and said, "Well, I suggest you figure this out quickly," and basically stormed out of my office. I won't say he slammed the door, but he closed it rather forcefully.

I was taken aback. My pulse had picked up pace. Nobody wants to be part of an exchange like that. So, I took a few deep breaths and thought about what I had said and how I had said it, why I had said it, and in the end, I felt good about my choices. I felt I was being fair. But I decided to give my favorite coach and confidant a quick call.

Julie said, "Is everything OK?"

I replied, "I think so, but I want to give you a scenario and hear your thoughts on how I responded."

She said, "Of course." Julie's always candid and supportive and conscientious with me.

I walked through everything with her and she said, "Carl, I totally support how you handled it. I think it was the right thing to do. You've always said that every time you say yes to something you're simultaneously saying no to something else, because we only have so much time available to us. And usually the no is to our workouts or time with our friends and family or whatever, and you have become masterful at being conscious with your yeses and nos. So, quite frankly, I'm disappointed in the way he reacted. And given how much you already give, I'm so sorry that you had to go through that. I think you already know what to do, which is to carry on, but check in with others, and then maybe circle back with him when you can."

I hung up the phone, and about twenty minutes later one of my peers came to my door and said, "Do you have a few minutes?" He was clearly distraught so I said sure. He closed the door, sat down, and his eyes started to well up a little. He said, "Sorry, I just need to compose myself. I don't know if I'm angry, frustrated, or scared. I just need a safe space."

I told him to take his time and kept doing some other things while he caught his breath. Eventually, he said, "You are not going to believe what just happened."

As it turns out, after leaving my office, the same partner went to see my friend and said, "This new project that came in. I thought we had someone else lined up but it looks like they're probably not going to be able to do it, so I was hoping you could take it on." Of course, my colleague knew nothing about my conversation with the same partner just a few minutes previously! And the partner basically told him that he expected that he would take the work on.

"Carl, you know I'm swamped, just like you are," he said. "I can't imagine how I'm going to take on one more thing! I don't know what to do."

I said, "So, what did you do?"

He said, "Well, I mean, come on, Carl, as if I had a choice! Obviously, I agreed. It's not like I could say no to him."

I said, "Frank, I need to tell you something." And I told him everything that had just transpired.

And he said, "Are you serious? You said no to him?"

I explained that I hadn't said an absolute no. But I had told him that I couldn't give a yes, not yet, and that I needed a little time to work it out.

Frank replied, "Oh my gosh, good for you."

I asked him how the partner reacted after he said yes, and Frank said he seemed happy about it. I added, "For what it's worth, you now have to figure out what you're going to do, but I strongly suggest you don't just pretend you can do all of it, because in the long run, not only is it unsustainable but I

"It's not like I had a choice."
Such phrases become the
norm when practiced enough—
until we break the pattern
and model otherwise.

think you're going to hurt yourself—the quality of your work, your commitments, your health."

"You're right," he replied. "I'm going to do what I should have done in the first place."

THERE IS one last twist to this story. The next morning I arrived early and the partner came into my office and asked me if I had a few minutes. I said sure, so he closed my door, sat down, and said, "I owe you an apology."

I said, "Thank you, I really appreciate that."

He laughed and said, "You haven't even heard what I'm apologizing for!"

I laughed too and said, "Fair enough. But thank you for whatever it is, and for making time to see me."

He said, "I don't know if you noticed or not, but I was pretty flustered and upset after you said no to me yesterday. OK, I know you didn't say no, but I kind of heard it as no. It upset me because, about two hours earlier in the day, that account was dropped on me. I had just finished venting to my wife about how much I had to do. So, I wondered if you were available. And when you handled it the way you did, I thought to myself, 'Holy shit, I should have said that to the senior partner who brought it to me.' Because you responded the way you did, I couldn't argue with you, so I was upset with myself for saying yes. I was upset at you for handling it in a way that I could have."

He ended by adding, "I want to thank you, because I think you taught me a very valuable lesson, and I want you to know that I'm very sorry, because I should have never handled myself that way."

I said, "Well, again, thank you for saying that. And by the way, have you been able to find anyone else to help?" I didn't say anything about Frank coming to see me.

He said, "Oh, I found someone else who is able to do it."

I said, "Well, before you leave, just out of curiosity, given everything that we've just talked about, the shared learning, which I celebrate, are you sure that person can take it on?"

The partner looked at me and said, "Why, did they say something to you?"

I said, "Maybe they did, and maybe they didn't. But are you sure that they just weren't afraid to say otherwise?"

He said, "I'm not sure, actually. I should check with them."

"That would be great," I said.

Then he added, "And if they need my support, I'll give it to them. I don't know if I'm going to tell them about my own lesson learned, but I can at least make sure they have the support they need. And you did see them, didn't you?"

"Maybe I did, maybe I didn't. But I don't think the point changes either way."

"No, it doesn't," he agreed. And then he shook my hand and off he went. I sat in my office thinking about how fascinating it was that my friend Frank had said, "It's not like I had a choice." The partner also modeled as if he didn't have a choice either. Such phrases become norms when practiced enough and then they become the repeated patterns—the culture—until we break the pattern and suggest (as well as model) otherwise.

The same partner came to see me about a week later and said, "I need you to help me become better at living our firm's values, because it is clearly a weakness for me." We did a lot of neat work together, and he's at the heart of the organization to this day. He's now a strong advocate for people speaking up. It's a nice story with a good ending.

IT BOGGLES my mind, the number of times in my career I've heard that phrase: "It's not like I had a choice." I know what people mean but it's so much more empowering to say, "I know I do have a choice and I'm still going to choose this." In other words, you might still make that decision but don't give up your power to choose, because otherwise, without even knowing it, you victimize yourself.

A power dynamic was at work in that story too. It had a political undertone, by virtue of the partner's formal seniority. Not only did I have to check myself but I had to call Julie to check in. And then Frank didn't feel like he could say no. If the relationship between the partner and me had been even better, more personal, we wouldn't have needed any of that adventure. I would have been that much more emboldened to say, "George, it's me! What do you mean? Just let me check into it and I'll get right back to you." No doubt he then would have come clean with his frustrations and thanked me before leaving. And he would have been more honest with me to begin with, and all would have resolved itself in one conversation. So back to "relationships are everything."

If I were to do that over again today with the experience I have now, as soon as I saw he looked frustrated, I probably would have called him on it and said, "I don't want to be the cause of any frustration. I'm happy to dive a little deeper here if that would be helpful." I would be a little more forthright with my intention, with picking up on his anxiety, and the path might have been easier to navigate.

That's part of what experience teaches you. If I see somebody struggling, now I am unlikely to leave it there. I will at least attempt saying, "I'm picking up on some frustration; I don't want to be the cause of that. Can we explore that a little and maybe I can help?" Sometimes it can help. If someone's already hijacked, it may not—they may just need some time. There's only one way to know for sure—give it your best shot.

More on Julie and Saying No

To go back to Julie and her lists, when I would hang up the phone, the thing I struggled with was "How do I say no to working late?" The way she would always voice it to me was "No, you have other commitments and they're not negotiable." That was her way of saying, "Since they're only seeing part of the story, they don't deserve your extra time." When the people on the left side asked me to work late, they knew there was a cost to the request: I wasn't going to be home for my family. If it wasn't urgent, they wouldn't ask, out of respect for Julie too. Whereas the right-hand list didn't show regard in that respect. They were only asking for themselves, without giving any thought to me. That's why she would say, "It is no. I'm sorry. You have to tell them I reminded you of a family commitment. It can't be tonight. If they need you, then go in earlier tomorrow. But you're not available this evening."

It was a beautiful way of supporting my right to say no. If formal leaders do not prioritize developing a supportive environment, one where people can feel safe in speaking openly and honestly, then over time, they won't get the advantage of their team's discretionary energy.

I shared this last thought at a recent conference and someone said, "Hey, we say that, 'discretionary energy'!"

I said, "Truth be told, every business owner would love for individuals who are paid for nine-to-five to find it within their own heart and self-motivation to invest discretionary energy in service of the organization. Who wouldn't want that? But you can't command it. I mean, you can, but it'll be short-lived. People will do it one or two or three times, beyond which they will think, 'No, I'm not inspired to want to keep doing this.'"

But when you have high-quality underlying relationships that are deep and meaningful, people want you to succeed and so they'll give you extra time.

The pandemic was interesting because a lot of businesses found that when you have great relationships, people will work even more. Which can be just fine, as long as it's not getting in the way of walks, good meal prep, a good night's sleep, and all your fundamentals.

HUMOR HAS a direct bearing on the quality of our relationships too. Being talented with humor—not inappropriate but effective with it—is a powerful gift. Find the light in the dark, if you will, and start with learning to laugh at yourself. At the end of the day, I know we're going to figure something out, so let's not take ourselves too seriously—and yes, there's science behind that too. Remember, playfulness, hopefulness, compassion, and mindfulness are the four modes of operation that trigger our parasympathetic nervous system, putting us in the state to access our best.

Over the years many of my friends and colleagues have been excellent at defusing situations with humor; it's always impressive to watch. But beware—not everyone has this strength. People naturally have different strengths, but the ones who are good at eliciting laughter make everything seem like it's going to be all right.

Us Against the Issue, Never Against Each Other

We take ourselves seriously. We really do. My dad has always had a phenomenal sense of humor and even at the end of difficult meetings, he would chuckle a little and say, "What do you say we go and have a nice dinner together now?" Or "Why don't we do this or that with the other coworkers?" That relationship orientation, that level of resonance, never waned, regardless of the topic at hand. It was always the team against the issue, never against each other, and he had this brilliant way of reinforcing that. Time after time I witnessed how his genuine, kindhearted laughter and humor disarmed even the toughest exteriors.

Once, at a charitable event our family attended, a board member of the company where my father worked asked me, "Aren't you Hugh's son?"

"Yes, very nice to meet you."

"I've got to ask you something. Is he like this all the time?"

To which I said, "I don't exactly know what you mean, but I have a good idea. The answer is yes."

"How does anyone punish someone like him?"

When my dad heard this later, he laughed, knew it was said in fun, and added, "Why in the world would you ever want to punish somebody? What's the objective there? What's the goal, the aim?" And then, "Are we making strides to close the gap between where we are and where we say we want to be, individually and organizationally? That needs to be the focus."

18

Leading Indicators to Celebrate

OW DO you measure success on a team or in business? In one of my former roles as a human capital leader, I was often asked this question. I would say, "What metrics matter to you, through the lens of your local office?"

And people would list their expected key results, either weekly, monthly, or quarterly.

I'd say, "Great. So, as long as you deliver on those, you're less fussed about how you do it? You're just more interested in the results."

They would invariably reply, "Absolutely."

This may sound very familiar. "Just get it done," as the saying goes. But consider, if this is your approach, that you might be missing an amazing opportunity to positively reinforce team members for progress made along the way. This preoccupation with results (lagging indicators) as opposed to the actions that lead to those results (leading indicators) might be costing you an ability to nurture the very culture you aspire to. It's little wonder why many teams share that they do not formally engage their organizational values when choosing their words and actions. Positively reinforcing the behavior we want to see more of is the best way to ensure it happens. If one cares only about the destination, the journey will often be made up of behavior that cuts corners and compromises others along the way.

When a team practices consciously living organizational values and makes decisions that align with the mission while focused on moving in the direction of the vision, the results will speak for themselves. By celebrating progress against leading indicators (actions) and recognizing others when they role model the best of your values, your lagging indicators (results) will very likely flourish. The now is in the how, and the more aligned you are moment to moment, the greater your synergy, momentum, and sustained productivity.

A friend of mine who had similar human capital responsibilities with one of our clients asked if she could observe the beginning of one of our office meetings. We had discussed the points above and she had indeed observed a variety of less than desirable behaviors arising out of a "results at any cost" mentality within her organization. She attended the introductory part of our meeting to see how we raised these types of insights.

After welcoming everyone and thanking them for their time, we began. "Good morning, everybody. We'll be revisiting our goals today. But first I wanted to say that, as we know, the best way to achieve our targets is with some fun, excitement, joy, and growth-orientation. We prioritize getting to know each other well and celebrating our unique strengths. As we learn about those strengths over time, we're going to deploy them consciously, tactically, in service of the strategies we develop together."

Our guest jumped in and complimented our team for their great energy, focused attention, and positive body language. She asked if someone else on the team would sum up how ongoing positive reinforcement was engaged among them.

A senior manager chimed in, "Who doesn't want to play to their strengths? As we progress against milestones and visibly try to live our values, we have fun celebrating one another. We provide positive shout-outs and thumbs-up cards, and ensure we're celebrating what goes well and when we overcome any number of challenges. If someone on the team takes on something significant, we also want to see them receive a bonus thanks to their impact. All to say, we care about one another and know that it's up to each one of us to show that every day. The end result: We have fun, enjoy our experience, and champion each other."

Our guest asked, "Does anyone ever want to leave this office?"

Everyone in the room smiled and collectively replied, "No!"

She stayed for a few more minutes, asked a few more questions, and finished with thanks and a request for any last thoughts.

A different manager spoke up, "Because of how we behave with one another, we often give extra time to the organization in pursuit of our goals. Our families know we're appreciated here, and they too are appreciated and celebrated at various events throughout the year. We end up wanting to give that much more to our team members, to make sure they're thriving in service of our clients and that they're doing well personally. Our excellent metrics end up being a by-product, because we focus on the leading indicators of success that drive those lagging indicators. But we do it consciously, through our coaching. We do it candidly and openly and honestly. If anybody is struggling, we shoulder the struggle together. Sure, we're going to call each other out if needed, but we do it supportively and with clear positive intent."

Having set the stage for celebrating success and not for policing failure, we would measure ourselves weekly against meaningful leading indicators and pay less attention to the lagging ones. And guess what happened? Take any time period you want and run the numbers by individual or by staff level or by territory, and our numbers were always at or near the top. We had the highest retention rates with the lowest amount spent on advertising, and traditional metrics involving profitability excelled too. We didn't have to advertise because we had more people who wanted to join our team than we could take. This all happened by design. By doing the things we've been talking about.

Of course, in this book I'm making it far more tangible to better show how we did it. I hope by now you are aware that you have to live it. The awareness part is huge. And then there's asking, "What do we do to make this better, consistently?" And guess what? The more consistently you make something better, the greater the odds it becomes a new habit. Show me your habits and I will show you your identity, the consistency of your beingness, your norms. And if you want tomorrow to be different from today but you're choosing the same behaviors, OK, but it's not going to be different. You've got to become consciously intentional.

You also have to be prepared. When I used to walk into performance review meetings, I was prepared to show all the ways that team member X delivered—supported by upward feedback, peer feedback, and client feedback. Look at the number of times they were asked to return to that client. Look at the number of new leads they got because the client referred them; look at the number of people who requested them as their coach. I connected all these dots and corresponding metrics in a way that celebrated that colleague and their impact, so their progress was visible and validated. There was nothing left to doubt about how each member of the team was important. We wanted everyone to feel and know that they mattered, that they belonged.

To return to the original question, all we care about is results, right?

Today, when a client asks me, "How are we going to know if you're making a difference?" I say, "Well, you don't need any new measures. Take all your existing ones. They're all going to get better."

They may say, "Which ones?"

"All of them."

"But over what period of time?"

"It doesn't matter. If you're serious about doing something with what we explore together, all your measures will improve."

The only one that might take a slight dip (initially) is around trust, because when people start to communicate new aspirational expectations, naturally there will be skeptics. Anyone who has been around a while often says something like, "Yeah, I've heard this before." But as soon as they see you behaving in alignment with your commitments, you will see people changing their attitudes—and you'll see the multiplier.

A simple truth is this: If you're difficult to be around, you will get what you ask for and no more. But when people enjoy experiences with you and become a better team member because of it, they're happy to make more time with you. That's what I called "discretionary energy" in the

Call each other out
if needed, but do it
supportively and with
clear positive intent.

previous chapter. People are mostly paid fixed salaries, and so the second somebody decides to give the company one more hour than what they otherwise would have given, it goes right to the bottom line. If they unblock someone who is upset or answer a call from a client in desperate need or cover for someone who has a family situation... the scenarios are endless, but that hour is only available because they chose to invest it. And they'll only do that voluntarily (and repeatedly over the longer term) when they're enjoying the experience and appreciated accordingly.

I've known many employees with a track record of working long hours. To them, I always offered, "Please only choose this to a point, because there are diminishing returns—we're human." I wouldn't allow them to work after so many hours if I sensed they were getting tired. No one could argue that energy of a higher quality, greater focus, and more intentional expression would better benefit the famed bottom line.

In *Tiny Habits*, BJ Fogg tells us, "Celebration will one day be ranked alongside mindfulness and gratitude as daily practices that contribute most to our overall happiness and well-being. If you learn just one thing from my entire book, I hope it's this: Celebrate your tiny successes. This one small shift in your life can have a massive impact even when you feel there is no way up or out of your situation. Celebration can be your lifeline."

Make Time for Coaching!

It's funny, so many people simply don't make time for coaching. There's still this cultural bias that a billable hour trumps everything else. So, in the presence of senior leaders and board members who declare that they are a billable-hours culture and ask me my thoughts about coaching, I say, "Well, we all know that an hour of coaching has a completely different value than an hour of chargeable time."

And they agree.

Notice how I worded that neutrally, without showing my hand. Then I say, "I mean, we all know that an hour of coaching is worth at least three, four, five billable hours, right?" And they just look at me because, of course, they were hinting that it's the other way around!

And I say, "Think about it. Say you've got a team member who is emotionally hijacked, depressed, or mentally struggling. And they're working on this marquee project with you and it's the eleventh hour and the pressure is on and they can't focus. And all you do is say get it done, because you're prioritizing that next chargeable hour.

"But instead, imagine if you decide to pick up on the cues and appreciate that we're human and that something is off, so you spend an hour with them, listen to them, and at the end of that successfully unblock them. They can now get back to what they were doing and they *want* to. Imagine the ripple effect this would have over the next three hours, five hours, or even a full day. Which gets a higher return, the traditional approach or one that includes needed coaching?"

I usually add, "If you're confused because you think it's too hypothetical, don't be. Just remember the last time you struggled with focusing on work, and then think of what helped you or could have helped you refocus. Or, by the way," I might say to someone I know well, "since you're a dear friend of mine, let's get even more specific: Can you think of a time when you were derailed and you called me? It has happened a few times. And we spent some time together. Tell me a little bit about what happened after we finished our talk."

More often than not, that person recounts specific situations of going into a meeting or in front of that client differently, with the courage to do something or have that challenging conversation with someone they had been avoiding...

I say, "Do you see how you can be a student of your own experience? Ten minutes ago you were arguing that a chargeable hour is worth multiples of one coaching hour. Now you see that the opposite is true. Is that fair or unfair?"

"Fair—totally agree," they say.

To which I reply by asking if they will make more time to coach people who need them.

"Yes, I will."

"OK, will you support that the organization value you for that time? I don't know that it will, but are you going to at least point out that, in your estimation, it must if it wants others to take hold of this new habit?"

The consensus has always been yes.

As we've also often heard, "When all is said and done, a lot more is said than done." But the ones who really make the difference say, "I will do that—the leader in me insists."

To which I say, "Beautiful."

19

The Virtue Compass

SPEAKING OF actions, I'm often asked how to choose what to focus on and when. What are the best actions to take, and how will you know?

In my personal and consulting work, I often use my Virtue Compass. This is how it works: No matter what's going on in life, no matter the challenge, the simplest question you can ask yourself is "Which of my favorite virtues can I practice, right now, in light of this challenge? If I'm going to consciously practice operationalizing my virtues, then first, I need to know what they are, and second, I need a challenge. Which virtue do I want to operationalize right now?"

The tougher the challenge, the greater our opportunity to practice. And daring to put that process in play bodes well for you and those in your midst. You're going to be much better off than somebody who has no concept of their values or virtues and so reacts rather than responds. The most consistently effective and inspiring leaders are guided by their virtues, regardless of the direction they choose to travel.

At a recent conference I attended, a participant said, "Wow, Carl, we all feel so equipped now to go slay dragons!"

I replied, "You know what? You really are slaying dragons on your hero's journey. Even in your mission statement you allude to taking on the world's toughest challenges. You are metaphorically slaying dragons, not merely sidestepping lizards!"

That got a big laugh.

I said, "Why do I point that out? Because it's not easy to slay a dragon. You might get a few bumps and bruises along the way, but you are moving toward something else on this journey that is so much more meaningful than the fear you face with that metaphorical dragon. And you know you're up to the task. That gets back to the etymology of the word 'hero,' which is 'protector'—it's having the strength for two. So, how do you evidence that?"

All these things come full circle. I wanted those leaders to remember that the next time it's hard, it doesn't mean they should acquiesce or curl up in a ball or make excuses or point fingers. When it's hard is when you say to yourself, "Awesome, I now get to practice one of my favorite values, and by putting it into action and realizing it, it will become a virtue. Now that is something I want to explore."

This work is about putting virtues into action. In *Flourish*, Martin Seligman says, "In authentic happiness theory, the strengths and virtues—kindness, social intelligence, humor, courage, integrity, and the like (there are twenty-four of them)—are the supports for engagement. You go into flow when your highest strengths are deployed to meet the highest challenges that come your way. In well-being theory, these twenty-four strengths underpin all five elements, not just engagement: deploying your highest strengths leads to more positive emotion, to more meaning, to more accomplishment, and to better relationships."

The most consistently effective and inspiring leaders are guided by their virtues, regardless of the direction they choose to travel.

What we're doing is helping each other, more often than not, to elevate our self-awareness, improve our self-regulation, and move toward our mastery. Practicing what matters most so that yesterday's best becomes today's new baseline—spiraling up, together.

Those are first principles. What it's all about. My hope is that the stories and insights that resonate most will last, become part of your best, part of your practice—and help the world meet (maybe for the first time) the radiant exemplar, loving optimalist, and encouraging essence that is you; the highest and most loving and effective experience of you. Let's act, together, and envision that sweet and fun day down the road when we meet: the quality of your energy, its focus, and how you express yourself, a joy to behold and magically memorable. The habit of you—a presence that cares, loves, respects, helps, and celebrates the best in others. The best ever conscious transformation from state to trait—that's you!

It doesn't matter where you are starting from. What matters is that you start—again and again if need be. It's always day one.

The Virtue Compass is the next chapter, which asks, now that we've got this in hand, this ability to be self-aware, to self-manage, self-regulate, self-lead, self-master, to what end? To the end of making sure we operationalize our top virtues in service of this moment.

The world needs your best—without it we will never know the possibility that could have been. The actuality that would have been.

Thank You

THANK YOU to my incredible wife, Julie, and my inspiring children, Scott and Haley. The three of you have, without a doubt, been my most consistently loving and encouraging supporters. Scott and Haley, when you asked me to please capture some of my experience in writing so that you could both have it and share it, the seed was sown. You three are my inspiration!

Michael and Marcella, let's be honest, this book would not have happened without you both. Your friendship, love, support, encouragement, challenge, and passion for seeing purpose through are what I needed, when I needed it. Michael, your lifelong coaching and introduction to the Page Two team has made all the difference—thank you!

Brian Johnson, I have no doubt you'll see your influence throughout these pages. From my coaching certification to the Heroic community that we all have the privilege to learn from on a daily basis, I owe them to the hero's journey you started so many years ago. Thank you, my friend—grateful for you.

To my Page Two family—wow, you are wonderful, thank you. From the day I met Jesse Finkelstein, I knew this was the publisher for me. Jesse, your kindness, competence, and sincere desire to see others succeed are remarkable. Scott Steedman, you were the first member of the team to take on helping me structure and edit our approach from the very beginning. Your experience, creativity, friendly prompts, and belief in the lessons being explored gave me confidence to keep going—thank you, my friend. Kendra Ward, my copyeditor, you were a joy to spend time with and to trade ideas with. Your approach was always welcoming, curious, nurturing, fun, and imaginative. I trusted you from the very beginning and feel so grateful to have had you as a partner—thank you! Adrineh Der-Boghossian, you're the reason we made it to and through the finish line (together), quite literally. As our project lead and my manager, you made the process understandable, manageable, fun, and engaging—thank you! Ariel Hudnall and Leonni Antono, thank you—for your kindhearted approach and ongoing encouragement, and for ensuring the world would learn about our work, guiding me through the communication, and helping our successful introduction. Madelaine Manson, your guidance, kind energy, and expertise will be the key to ensuring our book makes its way into as many hands as possible. You took a very complex distribution process and gave me every confidence that our customer experience will be seamless, easy, efficient, and tailored. I can't thank you enough! Jennifer Lum and Fiona Lee, wow, what can I say, your cover, interior design, and illustrations are beautifully crafted and on point. Taking the time to get to know me and then infuse what you learned into our collective work of art has been a joy to witness—thank you.

To my entire beautiful family, who provided the source of so many life experiences, stories, and lessons learned along the way, I remain thankful to you all, every day. Mom and

Dad, there are no words for what your love and guidance gives me—thank you!

Maggie Habieda, I am so grateful for your kind attention to detail, professionalism, and the fun we had capturing the photo of me that will forever be a part of this book. Your entire team was a joy to work with!

To everyone I quoted, please know that I chose you intentionally, to learn from and with you and to celebrate your wisdom in my own small way—thank you!

To those of you who have faithfully and consistently asked about the status of my book, and who requested any number of signed copies before I had even written it, I celebrate and thank you. You know who you are, and I can't wait to deliver it to you in person.

Finally, to two individuals who, other than my family, may very well have been first in line to celebrate this occasion: Paul Glover, my longtime mentor and friend, I think of you often, celebrate your kindness, and remember you fondly; and Kathy Conway. I did it, Kathy—your love, support, and belief in me are a gift that has now been made manifest—thank you, my dear friend. I miss you!

Selected Bibliography

THIS BIBLIOGRAPHY is not a complete record of the many insightful works and sources I have consulted in writing this book and in studying the biological aspects of leadership for some thirty years. I have gleaned much knowledge through workshops, conversations with experts, and in my own observations of my experiences. The list that follows represents sources you might turn to yourself, to continue your own exploration.

Blake, Amanda. *Your Body Is Your Brain: Leverage Your Somatic Intelligence to Find Purpose, Build Resilience, Deepen Relationships and Lead More Powerfully.* N.p.: Trokay Press, 2018.

Bowman, Katie. *Movement Matters: Essays on Movement Science, Movement Ecology, and the Nature of Movement.* Washington State: Propriometrics Press, 2016.

Boyatzis, Richard, and Kleio Akrivou. "The Ideal Self as the Driver of Intentional Change." *Journal of Management Development* 25, no. 7 (2006): 624–42. doi.org/10.1108/02621710610678454.

Clear, James. *Atomic Habits: An Easy & Proven Way to Build Good Habits & Break Bad Ones.* New York: Avery, 2018.

Covey, Stephen. *The 7 Habits of Highly Effective People: Powerful Lessons in Personal Change.* New York: Simon & Schuster, 1989, 2004, 2020.

Cuddy, Amy. *Presence: Bringing Your Boldest Self to Your Biggest Challenges.* New York: Little, Brown Spark, 2015.

Fogg, BJ. *Tiny Habits: The Small Changes That Change Everything.* Boston: Houghton Mifflin Harcourt, 2019.

Frankl, Viktor. *Man's Search for Meaning.* Boston: Beacon Press, 2006.

Goleman, Daniel. "What Makes a Leader?" *Harvard Business Review,* January 2004. hbr.org/2004/01/what-makes-a-leader.

Gupta, Sanjay. *Keep Sharp: Build a Better Brain at Any Age.* New York: Simon & Schuster, 2021.

Harari, Yuval Noah. *Sapiens: A Brief History of Humankind.* Toronto: Signal, 2014.

Hefferon, Kate. *Positive Psychology and the Body: The Somatopsychic Side to Flourishing.* New York: Open University Press, 2013.

Jantz, Gregory. "What Are the Freeze and Fawn Responses?" *A Place of Hope,* April 18, 2023. aplaceofhope.com/what-are-the-freeze-and-fawn -responses.

Kruse, Kevin. "What Is Leadership?" *Forbes,* April 9, 2013. forbes.com/ sites/kevinkruse/2013/04/09/what-is-leadership.

Porges, Stephen, and Deborah Dana. *Clinical Applications of the Polyvagal Theory: The Emergence of Polyvagal-Informed Therapies.* New York: W.W. Norton & Company, 2018.

Seligman, Martin. *Flourish: A Visionary New Understanding of Happiness and Well-Being.* New York: Simon and Schuster, 2011.

Siegel, Daniel. *Aware: The Science and Practice of Presence.* New York: TarcherPerigree, 2018.

Soosalu, Grant, and Marvin Oka. "Neuroscience and the Three Brains of Leadership." 2012. mbraining.nl/leiding-geven/neuroscience-and -the-three-brains-of-leadership.

About the Author

CARL OXHOLM is founder and CEO of Virtue Compass Inc. (VCI), which helps individuals and organizations alike optimize their energy and manifest their intention. Prior to creating VCI, he spent almost thirty years in a variety of leadership roles with PwC Canada, being among one of the leading professional services networks in the world.

As a senior equity partner, he led service teams with an exceptional track record spanning multiple industries. A lead partner on some of the largest national (and global) priority clients, he enjoyed testing the power of positive influence. As the firm's national leader of culture and leadership, he developed service offerings around enhanced emotional intelligence (EI), increasing one's capacity to cope and thrive amid growing demands and expectations. He is a Certified Optimize Coach and was his former firm's national partner coaching leader, where he led a faculty of professional external coaches, sat on several global steering committees, and was a founding member of both its charitable foundation and women in leadership programs.

Also a chartered professional accountant (CPA), Carl was recognized by his profession in 2021 as a fellow. The distinction of fellow (FCPA) formally recognizes CPAs who have rendered exceptional service to the profession and in their communities. Becoming an FCPA is the highest honor a CPA can receive. It is recognition by peers for exceptional leadership, competency, and stewardship.

As a keynote speaker, he shares practical insights derived from his many years of experience and the unique roles that he has enjoyed within the professional services industry. Oxholm has traveled the world providing talks and facilitating workshops that involve culture change, EI, and leadership development. Having helped numerous global companies, not-for-profit organizations, and professional associations alike, he often says that it is his privilege and pleasure to serve wherever needed.

Call to Action

I AM HUMBLED that you chose to read *The Biology of Leadership* and hope that some of the insights resonated and provided food for thought that you can now enjoy experimenting with. Following any keynote address and workshop that I've offered, the number one request I have received up until now has been to write a book that contains the insights shared here. It was your voice that fueled my energy in the service of writing this book. From my heart to yours—*thank you*!

As for next steps, here are the ones that are top of mind for me.

Let's Connect

Please visit my site: virtuecompass.com

Find me on social media:

X (formerly Twitter): @CarlOxholm
LinkedIn: linkedin.com/in/carloxholm

Share This Book

For more information on bulk purchases, custom orders, and discounts, please contact **orders@pagetwo.com.**

Share a post of a key takeaway from this book on your social media and tag #BiologyofLeadership.

Team with Me

Let's team together to optimize your most important next steps.

- Need and want a course for your team's development? I would be happy to work with you and your team to tailor a program that builds on the core tenets of *The Biology of Leadership.*

- Interested in keynotes or workshops? I love tailoring to build on the most important aspects of what you've read and incorporate what you need to energize and develop your personal and team leadership capabilities.

Post a Review

The second most consistent request I receive from clients is for reading recommendations. If you have received some value from this book and think that others might too, please post a review on your preferred online retailer, or scan this QR code and leave a review.

This book is also available in ebook and audio format. I read the audio version myself in the hope that I can convey my gratitude for the journey that informed the words, along with my excitement for the future that awaits our never-ending experimentation and joy.

www.ingramcontent.com/pod-product-compliance
Lightning Source LLC
Chambersburg PA
CBHW030458210326
41597CB00013B/720